The New-York Historical Society
A Bicentennial History
1804–2004

By Larry E. Sullivan
Preface by Louise Mirrer

The New-York Historical Society
New York City
2004

Published by the New-York Historical Society, in conjunction with Akashic Books
©2004 New-York Historical Society

Design and layout by Keith Campbell
Etching on front cover by Ernest D. Roth, 1939; commissioned by the New-York Historical Society.
Back cover map: "Plan of the City of New York from an actual Survey," drawn by James Lyne and printed by William Bradford, 1731; gift of John Pintard.

ISBN: 0-916141-11-X
Library of Congress Control Number: 2004114993
Printed in Canada
First Printing

New-York Historical Society
170 Central Park West
New York, NY 10024
www.nyhistory.org

Contents

*The New-York Historical Society
and Alexander Hamilton*

Preface

On September 8, 2004, photographers from magazines and newspapers throughout the city captured the image of the New-York Historical Society wrapped corner-to-corner in a giant, multicolored ten-dollar bill. The banner heralded the Society's bicentennial celebrations as it proclaimed the opening of the biggest, most ambitious exhibition of its 200-year history, *Alexander Hamilton: The Man Who Made Modern America.* Hamilton, the quintessential New Yorker, died the year the Society, New York's first museum, was founded.

In the days that followed, the celebration of the New-York Historical Society's bicentennial attracted the attention of very many people—including those gawking at the banner as they strolled along the west side of the park or waited in traffic on Central Park West. The evening of September 9, 850 guests, including Governor George Pataki, Mayor Michael Bloomberg, Secretary of Treasury John Snow, and thirty-three descendants of Alexander Hamilton drank champagne and walked through the 6,000-square-foot exhibition, marveling at the portraits of early Americans who dared to dream that their newly independent country would someday occupy a place of privilege in world politics, finance, and culture. The guests were astonished to see amassed in one place so many of the original documents that spelled out the thoughts of Alexander Hamilton—immigrant, economist, lawyer, journalist, and civil rights activist—the most "modern" of our founding fathers.

The next day, by 9:00 a.m., 300 visitors were waiting in line to see the exhibition. Many of them that day, and subsequently, remarked on the changes they saw at the Society. Even those changes that could be called purely cosmetic (refinished terrazzo floors and gleaming brass, for example) seemed to spell a new beginning for the Society. We became, all at once, an institution squarely in the mainstream of the City's cultural destinations; a place that could share in the accolades of both public and critic, and in the inevitable discussions about mission and direction that took place, in 2004, at all major institutions of culture.

We are pleased, on the occasion of our 200th birthday, to receive the praise of so many constituents. We are also ready to answer questions about where we are headed in the years to come. Our trustees took care, in anticipation of new leadership at the Society, to set down their sense of the future. And I, as the

Society's proud new president, can with confidence say that at the approach of our next milestone birthday:

- We will have realized our ambition of being *the* locus of public engagement in, and enjoyment of, American history, seen through the prism of New York, the country's first capital.
- We will have achieved our goal of becoming a research institution hospitable to the most active intellectual community of historians, who will find in our facility, collections, and setting in New York City one of the best research environments in the world.
- We will be known as an institution that encourages scholars to engage the broader public in learning about American history.
- Our galleries and library will showcase, on a permanent basis, the Society's outstanding collections of paintings, rare books, manuscripts, and decorative objects.
- Our public will be able to count on a "blockbuster" exhibition featuring an historical figure, group, or topic each year.
- Our reputation as an educational center providing curricular and extracurricular experiences for New York City schoolchildren will be secure, and our collections and exhibitions will be accessible to the broadest public possible.

Our exhibition on Alexander Hamilton is but one dimension of the celebrations we plan over the course of this 200th year. A series of smaller bicentennial shows will feature the many treasures held within the walls of this splendid institution, spanning the period from our founding to the present day. These shows are called, "History Made Here," in recognition of the history that we ourselves made in 1804 when we became New York's first museum, and the history made by those whose lives and times are recorded in our collections.

It is fitting that the first treasures exhibition, which features the Beekman family carriage and an exploration of social status in America, is called, "Arriving in Style." After a decade's hiatus, and thanks to the generosity of our trustees, visitors to the New-York Historical Society are once again arriving in style at our grand entrance on Central Park West. Our reopened door is also symbolic of our aspiration to reach as many and as varied a set of visitors as possible, with educational and public programs as well as social activities.

Fifty years ago, the last history of the Society mused about the institution's future, especially in a world whose innovations—e.g., the increasing use of the long-distance telephone for important consultations—seemed to challenge the privilege of an organization that thrived on written records. As we move forward fifty years later, we know that despite many innovations that have transformed the way in which we collect and preserve the events of the past, our ability to present history has in no way diminished. It was, for example, the brilliance of my predecessor, Professor Kenneth T. Jackson, that enabled us, in the midst of horror, to nevertheless recognize the history made on September 11, 2001, and to concern ourselves with thinking about how to record a tragedy of such immense proportions. With Herculean efforts sifting through the wreckage at Ground Zero, and many hours spent recording the oral history of survivors of that terrible attack, the New-York Historical Society now preserves for posterity the full dimensions of New York's worst day ever.

Thus, with pride in our achievements over the last 200 years and pleasure in this moment of celebration, we once again raise our glasses to repeat the toast that in 1854 evoked a sense of limitless possibilities for the future of history:

> The twentieth of November, 1804—the birthday of the New-York Historical Society: rich in its memories of the past and in its hopes of the future, may each return of this anniversary find the Society more abounding in its means, more active in its operations, and more extended in its usefulness.

Louise Mirrer
President and CEO
New-York Historical Society
October 2004

Chapter 1

Charting the Course
1804–1857

Thomas Jefferson
Painting by Rembrandt Peale, 1805
Gift of Thomas J. Bryan

The period after the American Revolution and the Constitutional Convention was a time of nationalist fervor when historical studies were cultivated as never before. The nation was taking stock of itself, looking for its history, but found few collected resources from which to formulate and record its collective memory. The country saw a great eagerness to write history and saw the past as something immensely important. To be sure, local pride played a part as well as the fact that many of the country's leaders had a stake in the New Republic's creation. But history at the time went deeper and farther than local consciousness. The art and literature of the time were dominated by the past. We need only think of the classical architectural style so loved by Thomas Jefferson in his design for the state capitol building in Richmond in 1789; William Thornton's Roman design for the national capitol in 1792; and Benjamin Latrobe's 1809 Baltimore cathedral modeled after the Roman Pantheon. As we move into the nineteenth century the Greek revival in architecture overtook the Roman designs, and then later came a Gothic revival. The same classical style can be seen in the paintings of the late eighteenth and early nineteenth centuries. Historic themes dominated in literature, from gothic tales through the historical novels and romances of James Fenimore Cooper, Washington Irving, James Kirke Paulding, and others. Shakespeare was the most popular dramatist, and gothic melodramas predominated on the stage. From 1800 to 1860, thirty-six percent of best-selling books in the United States dealt with history. In the 1820s three out of four of the most popular books were historical. The word "history" helped to sell books. The fruits of historical writing in the first decades of the nineteenth century may have been disappointing to some, but they laid the groundwork for the great Romantics who burst upon the literary scene in the 1830s and the more scientific historians of the last half of the century.

It was in this cultural context that the historical society movement began. To write great history, one had to go to the sources, the original documents, in order to uncover the past. Colleges and universities were not in the forefront of the movement toward a more sophisticated historical discourse. They were locked in traditional curriculums and made little scholarly headway until later in the century. Consider Jefferson's attempts to create the University of Virginia in the first third of the nineteenth century or what happened to the curriculum of Franklin's University of Pennsylvania in the latter part of the eighteenth century. History-minded citizens—amateurs in the best sense of the word—led the way to historical associations and professionalism in America. Prominent men met for camaraderie to talk about history, to explain (or justify) their roles in that history, and to collect the documents that would affirm their collective and individual identities.

New York was in the vanguard of this movement. Only Massachusetts, in 1791, established a repository for historical documentation before New Yorkers gathered and founded one of the greatest of the national historical societies. The leading light among these organizers was John Pintard. He and several other prominent gentlemen of similar credentials met on November 20, 1804 to found the New-York Historical Society, today the oldest operating museum in New York City, and until 1880, when the Metropolitan Museum opened its building in Central Park, the only New York City museum of national distinction. Pintard and his colleagues were determined to establish a museum and library dedicated to research in the history of America and, secondarily, of New York State. Toward this objective, the Society has attempted, through good times and lean, to maintain a true and steady course. The minutes of this 1804 meeting charted the course of the Society:

> The following Persons viz: Egbert Benson, Dewitt Clinton, Rev. William Linn, Rev. Samuel Miller, Rev. John N. Abeel, Rev. John M. Mason, Doctor David Hosack, Anthony Bleecker, Samuel Bayard, Peter Stuyvesant and John Pintard, being assembled in the Picture Room of the City Hall of the City of New York, agreed to form themselves into a Society the principal design of which should be to collect and preserve whatever may relate to the natural, civil, or ecclesiastical History of the United States in general and of this State in particular and appointed Mr. Benson, Doctor Miller, and Mr. Pintard a Committee to prepare and report a draft of a Constitution.

Item 2 of this Constitution of the Society, adopted on December 10, 1804,

Egbert Benson
Painting by Gilbert Stuart, ca. 1820
Gift of Robert Benson, Jr.

reiterated succinctly that the object was national and not particularly local. A broadside issued on February 12, 1805, and again on September 15, 1809, elaborated further on this collecting mission: "Our inquiries are not limited to a single State or district, but extend to the whole Continent . . ." Furthermore, the Society will collect "Manuscripts, Records, Pamphlets, and Books relative to the History of this Country . . ." as well as all printed material relating to the United Sates, and "various productions of the American Continent and of the adjacent islands, and such animal, vegetable, and mineral subjects as may be deemed worthy of preservation." It was a broad collecting mandate and one that would be difficult to control in lean times, but one that resulted in the treasure house of material that the Society houses today.

In 1804 one could realistically aim to collect the hemisphere's output of recorded knowledge, as well as specimens of natural history. The collecting mandate made it unique among institutions of the period. The Massachusetts Historical Society early on limited both its membership and collection policy, remaining foremost a research library and foregoing the museum functions that take up so many resources in both staff and space. The American Antiquarian Society, founded in 1812 by printer-bookseller Isaiah Thomas, was similar in character to the New-York Historical Society in that it focused on national American "antiquities"; but early in its existence it limited its collecting policy to early printed Americana. Thomas would play a role in the Society's history by giving the institution its first legacy. Upon his death in 1831, Thomas left his New York counterpart a collection of books and $300 in cash. When the New-York Historical Society celebrated its sesquicentennial in 1954 it amended its bylaws; but its collecting policy remained national in scope, with an emphasis on New York State and its role in national affairs (article 2).

The Society started out with a burst of energy. Egbert Benson, the first president, and Recording Secretary John Pintard, led the way with their call for materials to document the early history of the country and region. Not only did they desire to collect and save for posterity, but they also aimed to publish original source documents. As early as 1811 the Society published in its first volume of *Collections* documents relating to the early Dutch settlement in New York. The Society took the lead among institutions of the period in publishing these early records, many of the originals which would be lost or destroyed in the ensuing years.

Although the Society had energetic, historically minded officers and members, ready to collect, publish, and preserve, the early years were plagued by a woeful lack of space for collections. For an organization dedicated to collecting just about everything relating to American civilization, its ambition far outweighed its resources. For the first fifty-three years of its existence it moved between a number of rented or shared spaces, with no home to call its own. It had six such homes before erecting its own building on Second Avenue and Eleventh Street in 1857. Following the course of the Society's locations is like watching the march northward of New York's population. But finally in 1857 the Society had storage and exhibition space for the only public museum in the city. It soon discovered, however, that it didn't have enough space for what it had already, much less room for expansion. Great collectors don't let such things hinder their progress, but problems do ensue from lack of resources.

What did the Society collect in these early years? What was its direction? The early years saw a flurry of activity. The Society had a series of presidents of distinction in local and national politics, beginning with Egbert Benson (1805–1815), former member of the 1776 Provincial Congress, representative from New York in the first two United States Congresses, among other offices, and called second in legal learning "only to Hamilton." Following Benson for a short period (1816) was Gouverneur Morris, drafter of the Constitution; DeWitt Clinton (1817–1819), senator, mayor of New York, presidential candidate (1812), and governor of New York (1817–1821, 1825–1828); David Hosack (1820–1827), distinguished physician and founder of Bellevue Hospital; chancellor of New York and prominent legal scholar, James Kent (1828–1831); Revolutionary General Morgan Lewis (1832–1835); Peter Gerard Stuyvesant, great-great-grandson of Peter Stuyvesant (1836–1839); Peter Augustus Jay (1840–1842), eldest son of John Jay, and prominent in city affairs in his own right; Albert Gallatin (1843–1849), Thomas Jefferson's and James Madison's secretary of the treasury; and educator and philanthropist, Luther Bradish

(1850–1863). It was a distinguished line of presidents and their prominence attracted the most historical, philanthropic, and benevolent-minded New Yorkers to assist the Society in its groundbreaking endeavors in promoting history. Most of these early leaders of the Society were conservative and believed that a good citizenry is an educated one. And what better discipline to teach democratic values than history, with its examples from the past.

As prominent as these New Yorkers were, it was the first recording secretary, John Pintard, who was the early guiding force of the Society. Pintard was a quintessential benevolent philanthropist of the early nineteenth century. Born in 1759, Pintard was brought up by an uncle. He was a member of the College of New Jersey's (later Princeton) Class of 1776. During the Revolution he served as assistant agent for American prisoners. Before the age of thirty he was well established in the business, political, and social life of New York. His list of voluntary offices is impressive and indicative of the type of man he was: secretary of the New-York Manufacturing Society; first Sagamore (later grand Sachem) of the Tammany Society; and senior warder of the Holland Lodge of Masons. He was clerk of the Corporation of New York and city inspector; organized New York's first savings bank in 1819 and was its chief officer from 1823 to 1841; helped found the General Theological Seminary; revived the Chamber of Commerce; promoted the Erie Canal; organized the Society for the Prevention of Pauperism and the House of Refuge (the first juvenile reformatory in the nation); and actively supported Sailor's Snug Harbor, the Mercantile Library, and the American Bible Society. In 1817 he mentioned holding eleven positions in a variety of remunerative and non-remunerative posts. Pintard and his fellow philanthropists were active in just about every political and cultural activity in the city. This was the age of the enlightened amateur and they took an aggressive lead in organizing society in their own image. Not for another sixty to eighty years would we see the professionalization of many of these societies and activities.

The Society's 1805 appeal with its extensive list of desiderata, including books, pamphlets, and manuscripts relating to the "whole continent" resulted in few gifts coming in. John Pintard realized what most museum and library directors realize today—that great collections are built on strength. The Society as yet did not have a great library. Pintard was an inveterate book collector

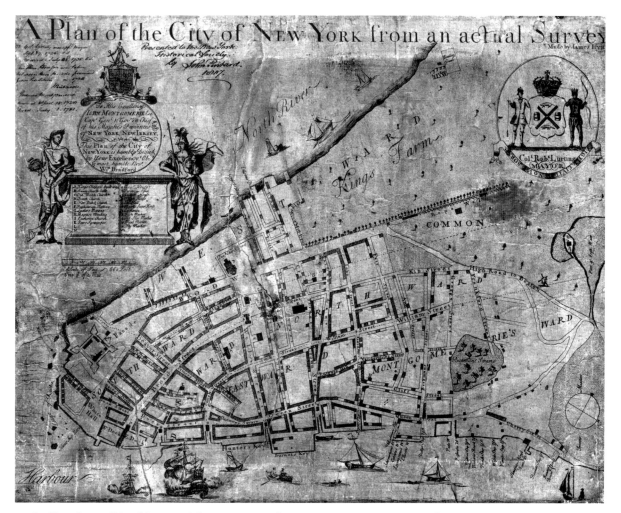

"Plan of the City of New York from an actual Survey"
Map drawn by James Lyne and printed by William Bradford, 1731
Gift of John Pintard

and offered to sell his library of Americana to the Society at cost. By 1809 the Society had raised some funds and purchased Pintard's extensive collection. (Thomas Jefferson would follow the same path when he sold his book collection to Congress after the British burned down its library during the War of 1812.)

By 1812 the Society recorded nearly 500 books and pamphlets, manuscripts, maps, and other rarities. Most of these were gifts from the Society's friends. Some of the most prominent of the rarities included the second edition of John Eliot's *Indian Bible* (1685); the first plan of New York City by James Lyne, printed by William Bradford, New York's first printer, and thus called the *Bradford Map* (1731); John Filson's *Map of Kentucke* (Philadelphia, 1784); the rare first edition of Joannes de Laets's *Nieuwe Wereldt* (1625); and Washington Irving's satirical *Knickerbocker's History of New York* (1809), which carried a dedication to the Society. Also in the first library catalogue was an entry for 209 issues of the first newspaper in America, *The Boston News Letter,* as well as William Bradford's *New York Gazette,* the first newspaper in New York. The emphasis on the collecting of newspapers is typical of John Pintard's view of historical sources. Early on in his diary entry for 1793, Pintard wrote this about newspapers: "To this source may be traced that general information on all subjects which peculiarly distinguished our citizens from the mass of the Old World. A newspaper comes to our fireside and its multifarious contents affords something to gratify the curiosity of every description."

The City of New York by Samuel Seymour
Engraving after painting by William Birch, 1803
The Accessions Fund

Here we see the beginning of the Society's great collection of early American newspapers, the fourth largest such collection in the United States. It is appropriate to see such a collection in New York, the site of John Peter Zenger's freedom of the press trial in 1735. The judge's account of this trial would find its way into the Society's archives later in the century.

The large and valuable manuscript holdings of the Society began to take shape during this formative period. In 1816 Pintard reported one of the most significant gifts the Society had ever received. Poet and diplomat Joel Barlow was the recipient of Revolutionary War General Horatio Gate's papers. When Barlow died his widow gave the collection to the Society, although Robert Fulton had physical possession. When he died, Mrs. Fulton turned the papers over to the Society.

At the same time, art was not ignored. The Society holds one of the largest portrait collections in America. The beginning of this collection started with John Dixey's presentation of his copy of Ceracchi's bust of Alexander Hamilton in 1809. To show its appreciation of John Pintard, the Society asked the prominent American artist John Trumbull to paint his portrait. In addition to this Trumbull painting, the Society in its early years obtained portraits of Gouverneur Morris, Ezra Ames, and an engraving of Chancellor Robert R. Livingston.

During this formative period, natural sciences took up much of the Society's collecting resources, not the least of which was space. The age was, we must remember, one of "cabinets of curiosity" relating to the natural world. In Europe the most enlightened rulers kept private museums of animal and geological specimens. The Society had DeWitt Clinton as president from 1817–1819, and Samuel Latham Mitchill and George Gibbs as members, all deeply interested in natural history. Clinton also, as governor, urged the passage of a lottery bill that would provide the Society $12,000. In anticipation of this money, the Society formed committees in 1817 for collecting zoology, botany and vegetable physiology, mineralogy and fossils, coins and medals, manuscripts, and books. They embarked on a vigorous pursuit of specimens through circulars and letters of appeal.

Success caused some consternation. So many natural history examples poured in that the Society had no space to keep them. In 1829 this collection was presented to the Lyceum of Natural History. This was the first instance when the Society realized that it could not collect the entire universe of knowledge but had to concentrate on the mission of research in American history, especially through the building of a research library. Pintard wrote to his daughter on June 27, 1817: "It is our object to make our Library one of research for all that is curious and valuable . . . [It] may become like the extensive

John Pintard
Painting by Samuel Waldo and
William Jewett, 1817
Purchase from the Louis Durr Fund

Libraries of the Old World inestimably valuable to the erudite Scholar. To have a hand in the foundation of such a Library will be, hereafter, no small praise."

But all was not peaceful at the Society as it was in debt and the lottery money was spent before it came in. The Society then sold its share of the lottery to Union College for $8,000 to pay debts, but a special committee formed in 1824 reported debts outstanding of nearly $10,000. Economies were attempted, the library was closed, but in 1825 the Society still owed $7,500. Proposals were floated to combine the Society's library with Columbia College, the New York Society Library, and the New York Athenaeum. Members attempted other associations and combinations, but all failed. Thus, in 1825 officers of the Society proposed to sell the library by auction. Such a suggestion brought an outcry, just as it would more than a century and a half later during the Society's financial problems in the 1980s and 1990s. On May 4, 1825, the newspaper *The Commercial Advertiser* ran an advertisement for the auction of the Society's books set for July 18 unless some "literary body" stepped forward beforehand and bought the entire collection. Two days later the *Commercial Advertiser*, quoting the *Daily Advertiser*, editorialized that "all feel mortified in the extreme, to see such a proof of public indifference toward an institution so necessary to the literary reputation of New-York. But this is not the only objection:—a great many of the books, and we believe some of the most valuable in the collection, were the gifts of gentlemen from their own private libraries, present with the noble object of securing them to the public . . ." It is interesting to note how the principle of not betraying the public trust in deaccessioning museum and library materials was firmly rooted in the public's mind even before the appearance of rational and focused collecting policies. Furthermore, it is evident that at this early period of its existence, the Society and its collections were recognized as valuable and not easily replaced, and for their contributions to the creation of a powerful and unique civic culture.

Only twenty years after the initial appeal for materials, the Society's library, if not the museum, was considered one of New York's treasures. The events surrounding the proposed dissolution of the collections also illustrate the value placed on all things historical at this time. America was searching for its formative past and did not have the European luxury of thousands of years of documents to serve the historical imagination. The Society's early aim to collect original sources anticipated the revolution in historiography that Leopold von Ranke was engendering in Germany. Ranke's *Zur Kritk neuer Geschichtschreiber* [Critique of Modern Historical Writing] appeared in 1824. We can only wonder if any Society members knew of this work at the time, but Ranke's emphasis on political and diplomatic history based on archival sources fit in well with the Society's collecting focus.

It was also the age of romantic historiography. America, building and improving upon the literary and philosophical methodological tradition of the great French and English historians, such as Voltaire, Hume, and Gibbon, produced the Romantic historians Washington Irving, Jared Sparks, George Bancroft, and William H. Prescott, among others. All needed original sources for their works. The new American historians would lay a greater emphasis on research and facts than on philosophy. They, like Ranke, would emphasize standards and the authentification of facts. Francis Lister Hawks would say in his *Contributions to the Ecclesiastical History of the United States of America* (1836–1939): "In estimating a new history . . . the first point , of course, to be settled is authenticity." Hawks's own book collection would become important in the history of the Society's collections. Great collectors anticipate scholarly trends rather than just respond to them, or as the French author Honoré de Balzac said in *Cousin Pons*, his novel on art collecting, "It's up to a collector to be ahead of fashion." And in its early years the Society was doing just that in its ambitious collecting efforts, and these efforts were not ignored.

In July 1832 James Madison, former president and Father of the Constitution, stated, "Such institutions [as the Society] will afford the best aids in procuring and presenting the materials, otherwise but too perishable, from which a faithful history of our country must be formed." It is not an exaggeration that the pursuit of history through the collecting and publishing of primary sources was the intellectual rage during the first half of the nineteenth century. Historical societies sprung up everywhere. In 1838 the New-York Historical Society took the lead in organizing a collective effort to promote historical research among the societies then in existence. By 1860 there were 111 historical societies, and the only state east of Texas without one was Delaware.

If the Society was going to lead the historical advance, it had to get its fiscal house permanently in order, and in that department its efforts were less than stellar. To go back to the 1825 crisis, the institution was in turmoil over the financial predicament; its charter expired; resignations ensued; and the officers held no meeting between June 14, 1825 and March 14, 1826. Governor Clinton then went before the legislature and recommended renewing the charter and providing financial aid. He stated: "Its collection of books, manuscripts, medals and maps, illustrative of the antiquities and history of our country, are very valuable and ought to be preserved for the public benefit." The legislature renewed the charter but state financial help was not forthcoming. The following year, 1827, the Society went to Albany again and this time encountered success, receiving a $5,000 grant. The library was saved and most of its debts paid, except the one owed to John Pintard for his collection. He was never paid, and he never appeared again at the Society.

In fact, most of the founding officers retired from the operations of the Society in 1828 and a new administration took over with the goal of putting the organization on a sound financial footing. Perhaps the most memorable events during these years, years marked by financial woes and transient housing, were the gift of the Baron von Steuben Papers (1778–1782) from Governor Clinton via the historian Jared Sparks, and its first cash legacy, $300 plus books from honorary member and founder of the American Antiquarian Society, Isaiah Thomas. Such legacies would play a large part in the future of the Society, indeed in the future of every cultural institution in the country; they feed the very lifeblood of preserving our historical memory. These two gifts were the only bright spots in the years 1832–1836, during which confusion, loss of interest, mounting debts, and lack of leadership reigned to the extent that no meetings were held for three years and the doors to the library remained locked. From 1836 until 1841 the Society moved twice and suffered, like most of America, through the Panic of 1837. The collections, however, were still regarded as peerless. When the Stuyvesant Institute on Broadway gave the Society free rooms in 1837, diarist Philip Hone remarked, "The library (which is the most considerable in this country in books and manuscripts relating to the history of the United States, particularly the State of New York) has been well and tastefully arranged . . ." The move brought a brief resurgence in the Society's activities. It held a series of lectures given by the leading lights of history at the time, including George Bancroft and Francis Lister Hawks. The semi-centennial of George Washington's inauguration in 1839 was a cause for a celebration, and the anniversary meeting brought in John Quincy Adams as speaker. But in 1839 the Stuyvesant Institute went bankrupt, and the Society was forced to move yet again. In 1841 New York University came to the rescue and gave the Society rooms in its new building on Washington Square in return for allowing its students to use the library. The Society would stay at the university until finally getting a home of its own in 1857.

Even during these years of turmoil, gifts of rare books, manuscripts, maps, and portraits kept coming in. Most notable of the art was Charles Willson Peale's portrait of Alexander Hamilton. In addition, the Society received funds from the legislature to begin copying and publishing its already great collection of manuscripts relating to the state's early history. It is also during this period that the library started limiting itself to collecting material from the two Americas, rather than the whole of natural and recorded history.

The 1849 annual report recorded the library containing 15,000 books and pamphlets, 1,400 volumes of newspapers, 2,000 maps, 15,000 manuscripts, plus coins and medals. This gathering made it the best American history collection in the country.

"The Winter-Cantonment of the American Army and Its Vicinity for 1783"
Map by Simeon DeWitt, 1783
Gift of Richard Varick DeWitt

The Erskine-DeWitt manuscript maps of American Revolutionary War sites came to the Society during this period. This collection is described as one of the most important donations ever received by the Society. Robert Erskine, appointed geographer to George Washington's army on July 27, 1777, worked for over three years on a series of maps that depicted sites in New York, New Jersey, Pennsylvania, and Connecticut. By the time Erskine contracted pneumonia and died in October 1780, he had completed sketches of over 100 maps on

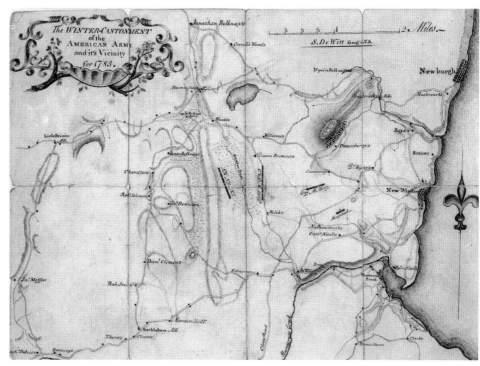

approximately 300 pieces of paper. Simeon DeWitt replaced Erskine as geographer after the latter's death. The maps, consisting mainly of plane table road surveys, passed into the hands of DeWitt's son, Richard Varick DeWitt, who donated them to the Society in 1845. These maps cover all the important battle and encampment locations in the above-mentioned states and are crucial to the study of the Revolutionary War. The collection is one of the Society's most requested resources.

Most importantly, throughout these years this collection was complemented with other maps of primary significance that made the collection necessary for any study of the Revolutionary War. See, for example, some of the maps drawn by the order of Sir Henry Clinton, commander of the British forces in America from 1778 to 1782. Most impressive is the "Map of the New York Island" drawn in 1781 by Andrew Skinner and George Taylor, official British cartographers on Clinton's staff. The names of large property owners are included and "the Plantations of Rebels are marked with the letters R.P." It shows Manhattan in detail and is a companion to another Society map holding that depicts New Jersey, New York, and Long Island.

Another Revolutionary War map of significance is neither American nor British but was made for the use of French officials when they were deciding whether or not to support the American colonies in the war against England. This "Plan de la Position de l'Armée sous l'Ordre de sa Excellence Lieutenant General Bourgoyne à Saratoga . . ." is the most detailed contemporary map of the Battle of Saratoga on October 10–17, 1777. Appropriately enough the library also holds in its Gates collection of manuscripts the original terms of convention that General Gates and "Gentleman Johnny" Burgoyne signed after the battle on October 17, 1777.

Given that Saratoga was one of the turning points of the Revolution, these documents take on great import for interpreting and describing the War for Independence. Perhaps it is difficult to fathom the importance of these collections today, when we take for granted such great repositories of manuscript Americana as the Library of Congress, which holds papers of the first twenty-eight presidents, as well as large collections of Revolutionary and Civil War primary sources; or the National Archives, which is responsible for presidential papers from Herbert Hoover on. But in the first forty-odd years of the Society's

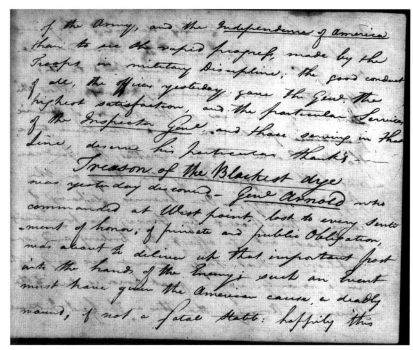

"Treason of the Blackest dye"
Report of Benedict Arnold's treason,
Revolutionary War Orderly Book
entry, September 26, 1780

existence it acquired the papers of such significant Revolutionary War figures as Horatio Gates and Baron von Steuben. Not many other institutions took their collecting mission so seriously and acted so energetically in the interest of recording the nation's past.

It was during this period that historians were writing about and forming our national historical consciousness. At their disposal were these collections. The significance of Gates's victory at Saratoga is now subject to modern revisionism, but for over 200 years it was taken as the turning point in the war, the one that brought the new United States respectability in the world of foreign affairs. And it was Gates who, after Saratoga, would for a short time rival Washington as the leading general of the Revolutionary effort. And take Baron von Steuben. Now unmasked as a bit of a fraud and not a "Baron" at all, he was one of the primary players who made the Revolutionary army into a real fighting force. He did this with his knowledge of Prussian drill and basic training, as well as how discipline and marching could win battles and how inspections could be positive rather than just disciplinary measures. He did such a good job that soon after his arrival on American soil Washington made him Inspector General of the Army and had his training manual translated from German into English. It is not going too far to say that historians would have a very incomplete picture of our struggle for independence without such collections to draw on.

In 1848 the Society received from Dr. Nathan Jarvis a collection of artifacts of the Plains Indians, as well as some South American materials. Wisely, these were later turned over to the Brooklyn Museum. The following year serendipity struck the Society when its librarian Jacob B. Moore resigned his position to become the first postmaster of San Francisco. Jacob's son, George H. Moore, succeeded him as librarian. Having an avid collector and loyal friend of the Society in California at this exciting time was a most fortuitous circumstance. Jacob sent thousands of maps, newspapers, ephemera, pamphlets, and prints back to the Society. Even before the great San Francisco earthquake and fire of

1906, which destroyed so many of the city's nineteenth century research materials, the Society held the finest collection of such materials in the East. Today it has one of the best Gold Rush newspaper collections in the country. Some of the very important rarities the loyal former librarian sent east were Harrison Wheelock's *Guide and Map of Reese River and Humboldt* (1864); "Map of the Gold Regions of California compiled from original surveys by James Wyld, Geographer to the Queen and Prince Albert," 1849; and H.S. Tanner's "Map of California, New Mexico, Texas . . . ," 1849.

Manuscripts and books kept coming in. A collector's item of inestimable rarity came in the form of the original 1670 Indian deed for Staten Island. But for historical researchers into the events leading up to the Revolution in New York, freedom of the press, and numerous other defining events, the papers of Daniel Horsmanden proved much more valuable. Horsmanden was an early player on the side of the DeLancey faction against the Livingstons in New York politics. His choice promptly brought rewards in the form of a seat on the Council in 1733, and an admiralty judgeship in 1736. Daniel Horsmanden was the chief justice and presiding judge over the famous John Peter Zenger trial in 1735, long seen as establishing the principle of freedom of the press in America, not to mention the act of jury nullification. Horsmanden's papers contain an account of this famous trial. Later James DeLancey went after the colonial Governor George Clinton, and after losing the battle, Horsmanden paid the price by forfeiting his offices in 1747. Historians of the first half of the eighteenth century also know him as the author of *A Journal of the Proceedings in the Detection of the Conspiracy Formed by Some White People, in Connection with Negros and other Slaves* (1744). This book (a first edition is in the Society's library), related the events of the so-called Negro Plot of 1741, and intended to caution as well as rouse the whites against the African-Americans in New York. Horsmanden came back into good graces in 1755 and became chief justice in 1763, did not fare well during the events of 1776, and finally died in 1778.

Some of the first William Bradford imprints came to the Society during the late 1840s. William Bradford (1663–1752) was the first printer in both Philadelphia and New York. He set up business in Philadelphia in 1685 and then owing to problems with the Quakers moved to New York in 1693. In 1725 he started New York's first newspaper, *The New-York Gazette*. Collectors refer to his early imprints as the incunabula of New York printing. Early Bradford imprints would become exceedingly rare and whenever the Society had a chance to acquire them it did with alacrity. A major treasure trove of these imprints, some unrecorded, came to the Society in the 1970s and 1980s and will be described when we near the end of our collecting story.

The defining moment during the first fifty-three years of the Society and our end point for this chapter is the acquisition of a permanent home, which the Society moved into in 1857. In 1850 Luther Bradish became the Society's tenth president and remained in office until 1863. America saw much activity during this period. California became a state in 1850; the Kansas-Nebraska Act was passed in 1854 and helped lead the country into civil war; the Panic of 1857 caused great suffering; and the outbreak and early slaughters and deprivations of the Civil War itself tore the nation asunder. It was a busy and wrenching time for the United States, but the Society came into its own during the same years. In 1851 gifts and the sale of publications resulted in the Society paying off all its debts. The Society gained a fiscal respectability and responsibility that it would not lose until the events of the late 1980s that almost resulted, as in 1825, in the downfall of the institution.

One of the great boons to the Society's collecting growth was in procuring the services of George H. Moore as librarian in 1849. Moore succeeded his father Jacob when the latter went to San Francisco. Heretofore the librarian occupied an unpaid position, but the Society began paying Moore $1,000 per year for his services. Moore served the library until 1876 when he became director of the Lenox Library, the precursor of the New York Public Library.

The year 1854 saw the Society's fiftieth anniversary, and, as the new building was assured, the future looked bright. The most noted historian of the

An example of the Society's rich collection of California Gold Rush material
Placer Times, *Sacramento City* December 15, 1849

period, Harvard's George Bancroft, gave the anniversary oration, and a procession of 3,000 members and guests arrived at Niblo's Garden Theatre at Broadway and Prince Street to the music of Bellini's opera *I Puritani*. (Proprietor and member William Niblo would become important to the Society's rare book collections in the future.) The *New York Times* reported that Bancroft's hour-and-a-half speech on the progress of the human race was much too abstract to resonate with the public. Perhaps the *Times* reporter missed or forgot some of Bancroft's more salient points because his talk was followed by a sumptuous dinner with numerous toasts that lasted well into the night. The *Times* summed up the event saying, "The celebration as a whole went off admirably."

Luther Bradish's greatest achievement was in building the Society's first permanent home where it would stay until moving into its present location on Central Park West in 1908. The building committee of the Society chose a lot on the southeast corner of Second Avenue and Eleventh Street, then one of the premier residential sections in the city. Through gifts and the legislature's exempting the Society from taxes, sufficient funds were obtained to build a handsome Italian-Doric style building, 55-by-92 feet with two stories, which opened in 1857. On the second floor was the library with an ample, domed reading room. John Ward Dean in *The Historical Magazine* described the library and museum components as such:

> Ascending a broad iron staircase, we come to the Library and Art Gallery, which occupy the remainder of the building. The vast apartment devoted to these objects is admirably planned and finished. The proportions are good; the alcoves and shelves are durable and elegant; the decorations in white and gold are chaste and pretty; and an abundance of light is let in from above. The floor is occupied exclusively by books; the first gallery by maps, charts, engravings, and American newspaper files, of which the Society has the largest assortment in the country; and the second gallery by pictures. The collection of paintings is one of the best exhibited in the city . . .

Perhaps most importantly, for the first time the Society had room for its collections. But the new building attracted more gifts, especially of art works, and soon it had run out of space again. But the new building did help the Society focus on certain areas of American art and not just accept whatever came its way. On the Society's 100th birthday celebration in 1904, the president mentioned that although the library saw tremendous growth in significant research material pre-1857, "museum growth was slow . . . probably owing to frequent moves and much that was given were specimens of natural history, which though acceptable as specified in the charter, were nevertheless unpopular with the members and consequently soon disposed of." That would change before long as the Society entered a new age of collecting art and research materials.

Chapter 2
Taste and Collecting 1857–1908

With the opening of the new building on Second Avenue in 1857 under president Luther Bradish (1850–1863), the Society was much better poised to take on the role as the leading museum in New York. Its home for the preceding half-century was a succession of shared buildings with little space to expand. Collecting art works was haphazard at best. But with new space, the Society for the first time had the facilities to expand, and at a dazzling pace. This was also the beginning of the age when men of wealth began forming the large collections and fortunes that built the great art and research institutions of today. The Morgans, Vanderbilts, Astors, Fricks, Lenoxes, and many other lesser known names plunged into the art and book market in a heroic way and changed the collecting culture in America. The New-York Historical Society was the fortunate beneficiary of many of these new cultural patrons, and it was during this period that its collections made the Society, for a time, the number one museum in New York and the country. From the opening of the Second Avenue building in 1857 to the final move to Central Park West in 1908, the Society grew at a frenetic pace as it purchased and accepted gifts of large collections. The Society's very success in this area would cause it troubles in the next century when both space and funds to care for the collections would become scarce.

In the first half-century of the Society's existence, art collecting was marked by the acquisition of single portraits and other artifacts that trickled into the museum collections. The opening of the Second Avenue site effected a striking change, both qualitative and quantitative, in collection building. The Society took its first initiative in accumulating large art collections and transformed itself from a somewhat amateurish (in the best sense) collector to New York's museum behemoth which attracted media attention to "blockbuster" collections. To be sure, the books, newspapers, and manuscripts relating to the study of American history still poured into the library, but for the first time in the Society's existence, art took on a significance and importance of its own.

We must not think of art collecting or even exhibitions of art as we do today. The "art" of collecting and exhibiting contemporary work was still in its infancy, even in the great capitals of Europe which sat on centuries of old masterpieces. The French began contemporary art exhibitions in the seventeenth century under Louis XIV when his minister Colbert instituted the "Academy" exhibitions at the Grand Salon of the Louvre in 1667. But not enough art was produced for them to become a regular occurrence until 1737. In England the first fully organized public exhibition of art took place in London in 1760. The initiative for this exhibition was taken by the artists themselves. The artist's position in Europe (and in America) at the time was one of subservience to patrons. The great majority of paintings were the property of picture dealers, their principal employers, who held artists in a type of vassalage. Exhibitions could make their names, therefore make them collectible, give them independence, and ensure a market price for British works of art commensurate with their worth. The 1760 exhibition was so great a success that 6,582 catalogues were sold, and it probably attracted 20,000 visitors. The chief significance of the 1760 exhibition is that it instituted the custom of annual public displays of art. The exhibitors and artists found that the general public was willing to pay for the enjoyment of art, and artists found a way to improve their financial position without accepting the subservient position implied in personal patronage. Not that the latter ended—by no means—but the artist at least had another outlet for his wares. In short, art became mediated by the market, for the benefit of the artists.

America followed this pattern early in the nineteenth century in the establishment of museums and art galleries, in the patronage of artists, and in the development of a market for art. The very real difference was that Americans and the adventurous collectors among them were new to the art collecting game and had many vast empty wall spaces to cover in their new, immense mansions. Americans did not have traditions of centuries of art to compete with, as in Europe. The European contemporary artists were vying for space with their ancestors, but Americans did not have that collecting base in place. To be sure, rich Americans bought European art and later in the century we would see a major collecting effort on a scale not seen before with the activities of the Fricks, Morgans, Huntingtons, and the like. In the early nineteenth century American collectors began acquiring the works of American artists. But taste changes slowly. First, however, Americans had to get beyond their infatuation with copies of European masters and traditional European patterns of collecting natural history specimens for their Cabinets of Curiosity. The Philadelphia artist Charles Willson Peale built a museum in Philadelphia in

The Course of Empire:
The Consummation of Empire
Painting by Thomas Cole, 1836
New York Gallery of Fine Arts

the late eighteenth century on the European model, filled it with natural history specimens, and created the model for early American museums. His self-portrait of 1822, *Artist in His Museum*, in the Pennsylvania Academy of Fine Arts, or the Society's own 1824 Peale, *Self Portrait with Mastodon Bone*, illustrate well the type of museum Peale created and his encyclopedic interests. New York had at least two such institutions in its formative years: the American Museum and the Columbian Gallery of Painting. To fill their wall space, many rich collectors would send artists to Europe to copy works from the European art canon. Thomas Jefferson, for example, thought it a mark of the connoisseur and educator to own copies of the European masters, as well as plaster casts of classical sculptures. Prominent New Yorkers such as Philip Hone and Samuel Ward sought European works and copies of the masters. It took Jefferson decades to appreciate original contemporary American paintings, but Hone began collecting Americana earlier in his collecting career. When Hone's collection of paintings was sold at auction in 1852, approximately one-quarter of his 125 paintings were contemporary American. These he cherished the most, exclaiming that the American works were "of artists now living, and I do not know of a finer collection of modern pictures." And Samuel Ward commissioned American artist Thomas Cole's series of four paintings, *The Voyage of Life*, now in the Munson-Williams-Proctor Institute in Utica, New York. Ward's hiring of Cole was most likely prompted by New York businessman Luman Reed's commission of Cole's *The Course of Empire*. Cole, one of early nineteenth century America's most prominent painters of the Hudson River School, never could break out of the patronage model. Not born to wealth, for most of his life he was dependent on a series of patrons for his livelihood. Most prominent among his benefactors were the Baltimore merchant Robert Gilmor and New Yorkers Stephen Van Rensselaer, Philip Hone, Samuel Ward, and Luman Reed. It was through Reed that the New-York Historical Society became the major player on the New York art scene for much of the latter half of the nineteenth century.

Luman Reed was a prominent businessman in the dry goods trade who amassed a great fortune after the War of 1812. It was during this period that Reed cultivated a taste for the arts. He joined the Sketch Club (predecessor of the Century Association), formed by "artists, authors, men of science and lovers of art." Included among the members were such artists of genius as Cole and Charles C. Ingham. Members met for discussions of "the sublime," "the emotions," "character," and "the nature of clouds." It is likely that Reed's cultural persona was formed during the 1820s and led him to art collecting on a grand scale. Among those influencing his artistic taste was certainly the above-mentioned Philip Hone, who was particularly taken with American artistic style and subject matter. Hone was a wealthy businessman and mayor of New York. Although his art collecting is what interests us at this juncture, he is best known today as the author of a famous twenty-eight-volume diary about New York City life, which he kept from 1826 until his death in 1851. This manuscript diary, one of the primary sources of New York City life, came to the Society during the Samuel Verplanck Hoffman presidency in the early twentieth century and has been mined for information by historians ever since. Because of

*Self-portrait by Thomas Cole, ca. 1836
Purchased from the John Jay
Watson Fund*

this magnificent resource, it is rare to see a history of New York about the first half of the nineteenth century without a mention of Hone.

Reed's business success enabled him to build for his family one of the finest residences of its day. The house, at 13 Greenwich Street, had three stories in the neoclassical tradition, and was completed in 1832. Reed devoted the third story to his fine collection of paintings, which he commenced to buy in 1830. By the time of his death in 1836, the collection numbered over fifty paintings, two-thirds of which were by contemporary American artists. Not only was Reed fairly unique in his time for his emphasis on American art, but he was highly individual among the wealthy art collectors in New York for making his gallery accessible to the public one day a week. Some evidence exists that he was the only New Yorker to open up his collection at the time, although the practice was common in Europe.

Reed also collected traditional natural history specimens for his Cabinet of Curiosities, facsimiles of Greek, Egyptian, and Etruscan vases, and a large collection of engravings, mostly of European masters. The latter were acquired for study, providing European styles, historical figures, and landscapes. He also acquired a library to aid him in his art studies. Reed died in 1836 and the New York Gallery of Fine Arts was founded with his collection in 1844. For a few years the collection was shown at the Rotunda in City Hall, and then the at the Academy of Design, before it was deposited at the New-York Historical Society in 1849. In the spring of 1858, following the 1857 opening of the new building, the collection was donated to the Society. This was the first large and coherent collection that the Society acquired, and it gave the art museum respectability and prominence to complement its invaluable research resources in American history.

What did the Reed collection include that made it so noteworthy? Between seventy-five and one hundred paintings, as well as numerous prints and sculptures were added to the Society's museum collections with this gift. Reed was a patron of a number of the most talented American artists of the period. We have already mentioned Thomas Cole's *Course of Empire* of 1833–1836. Two additional Cole paintings transferred to the Society included his 1833 *Sunset, View on the Catskill; Landscape (Moonlight)*; and his Salvator Rosa–inspired *Autumn Twilight, View of Corway Peak [Mount Chocorua], New Hampshire* of 1834, among others. These landscapes by Cole capture the essence of the artist's compositional creativity and picturesque romanticism.

Reed's collection also included several portraits and other paintings by Asher Durand. Durand, who was an engraver early in his career, first came to prominence with his engraving of John Trumbull's *Declaration of Independence*. He turned to oil painting exclusively in 1835 with the encouragement and friendship of Reed. Reed obtained the 1835 portraits of George and Martha Washington (after Gilbert Stuart), as well as Washington's successors, John Adams, Thomas Jefferson, James Madison, James Monroe, John Quincy Adams, and Andrew Jackson. Also in the collection is Durand's genre historical painting of 1835, *Peter Stuyvesant and the Trumpeter*. Durand turned to landscape painting in 1837 after a trip in the Adirondacks with his friend Thomas Cole. When the latter died in 1848 Durand became the undisputed leader of American landscape painting.

Reed was also a patron of William Sidney Mount. Mount was a genre and portrait painter who studied at the National Academy of Design. His most popular paintings were those with scenes of farm and country life. He was also the first American painter to sympathetically portray African-Americans. Reed's sponsorship of Mount resulted in a number of paintings in the gallery, including the first two works that Reed commissioned in 1835, *Undutiful Boys* (also known as *The Truant Gamblers*) and *Farmer's Bargaining* (better known as *Bargaining for a Horse*). Other pieces of stature in the collection included George Whiting Flagg's *The Chess Players*, ca. 1836, notable for the prominent presence of an African-American

The Chess-Players—Check Mate
Painting by George Whiting Flagg, ca. 1836
New York Gallery of Fine Arts

woman, with a much larger presence than in some of Mount's famous paintings. These commissioned and collected paintings illustrated the artistic prescience Reed had, and with the gift to the Society, it attracted other gifts of valuable works. A fundamental principle in institutional collecting is that one builds on strength and that the richness of collections attracts other gifts. And with the New York Gallery of Fine Arts collection finding a home in the Society's new building on Second Avenue, the Society held first place among museums in the city. It is also at this period that large art exhibitions became a Western cultural phenomenon. In 1855 the Paris International Exhibition had a special gallery of art works, and the Art Treasures Exhibition in Manchester, England in 1857 was the largest loan exhibition of art up to that time. With a building covering more than three acres, it attracted over a million spectators. This exhibition proved that good paintings on exhibit for a limited time would draw in a great number of spectators. Thus, 1857 was something of a turning point in the art world, and the Society was ready to play its part in the American art scene.

The next year James Lenox gave the Society an exotic and unique gift, at least in terms of size and weight. Lenox's father Robert was a wealthy merchant who was president of New York's Chamber of Commerce from 1827 until his death in 1839, when he was listed as one of the five wealthiest men in the city. James Lenox (1800–1880) used his huge inheritance to become one of the most prominent book and art collectors of the nineteenth century. For most of his life he collected on a grand scale, amassing a magnificent assortment of books (Americana, incunabula, Shakespeariana, Bibles), marble busts, paintings, engravings, and curios. Lenox and his Rhode Island counterpart, John Carter Brown, were the first American collectors to enter the European book markets on a large scale and compete with the English collectors and booksellers on their own terms. Both assembled magnificent collections of Americana. In 1847 Lenox was the first American to bring a Gutenberg Bible to America (for the "mad" price of $500!). He erected a large building on Fifth Avenue between Seventieth and Seventy-first Streets (now the Frick Museum) to house his collection. At the end of the century (1895), his library and endowment, along with that of John Jacob Astor and the Samuel Tilden Trust, would form the great New York Public Library. Lenox's career presents a good example of the wealthy collectors of the nineteenth century who built collections on an heroic scale.

Lenox's main book dealer was Henry Stevens of Vermont, and through Stevens he bought thirteen massive marble bas-reliefs from the Sardanapalus Palace in Nineveh. Lenox then donated these Assyrian marbles to the Society in 1858. So heavy they could only be placed in the basement of the building, they brought great prestige and publicity to the Society. Only the British Museum and the Louvre had similar examples of art from Nineveh. (Lenox would also present the Society with a copy of Shakespeare's *Third Folio* [1664].) In the same year Dr. Henry Abbott, a British physician who had been exhibiting his large collection of Egyptian antiquities in New York since 1853, attempted to sell these rarities for $60,000. Members of the Society, especially Frederic de Peyster, mounted a campaign to raise the necessary funds. They were successful, and in 1860 the largest and greatest collection of Egyptiana in America at the time was placed in the Society, and it went on view in 1861. (Although transferred to the Brooklyn Museum in 1937, it is still in the top tier of Egyptian collections.) This splendid gathering included 1,100 items with many outstanding examples of Egyptian sculpture, jewelry, and, for sheer viewer delight, three mummified bulls representing the Sacred Bull, Apis. Supposedly these are the only such specimens in the world.

World famous collections like the marbles of Nineveh and the Sacred Bulls caught the public's attention, not to mention great newspaper publicity. It is not exaggerating to say that the Egyptian collection represented the first "blockbuster" art exhibition in New York. It is too easy to use hindsight to criticize the Society about accepting these marbles and Egyptian artifacts. But at the time, the collecting scope was encyclopedic and the Society filled a very real need as a repository for these pieces. Obviously outside the field of Americana and eventually placed with collections and institutions contextually more appropriate, these items helped put the Society on the public map of cultural institutions and drew attention to the other great collections residing on Second Avenue.

The other large and significant collection that came to the Society during the Luther Bradish presidency was uniquely American and remains to this day one of the prized jewels in the crown of American art. John James Audubon began painting his monumental series of birds around 1810 in Henderson, Kentucky. When negotiating a subscription to Alexander Wilson's *American Ornithology*,

Wild Turkey (Meleagris
Gallopavo)
*Watercolor by John James
Audubon, 1825
Purchased from Lucy Audubon*

Audubon's business partner resisted a purchase on financial grounds while insisting that Audubon was a better artist than Wilson. (Audubon's actions at the time did not make him a friend of Wilson, nor did his subsequent dealing make him a favorite with many other American contemporaries.) After Audubon's bankruptcy in 1819 he took to painting an ornithological folio, which eventually resulted in 435 paintings of birds of America. The life-size paintings were to be turned into a subscription set of double-elephant folio engravings. Not finding a publisher in America, he turned to England, and eventually to Robert Havell, who turned out four volumes between 1827 and 1838. Late in life Audubon fell into senility and died in 1851. His sons, who collaborated with their father both in the artistic and business production of his books, especially the *Ornithological Biography* and *Quadrupeds of North America*, suffered business reverses and both died in the early 1860s. Audubon's widow Lucy was in severe financial straits and looked for a buyer for the original watercolors of *Birds of America*. The British Museum was interested and this treasure was in danger of leaving American shores. But Frederic de Peyster, who was so instrumental in obtaining the Egyptian antiquities, went to work again and raised the necessary $4,000 asking price, and this invaluable prize of American art came to the Society. The Society bought 433 of the original 435 watercolors (two were lost) and they remain a highlight of not just the Society's art collections, but also of American art and ornithology in general.

It is hard to imagine today the astute business deal the Society made with Lucy Audubon. Many of the original paintings of these birds would sell today (if ever offered) at well over one million dollars. Even some of the individual prints attain these lofty prices at market today. As for the Havell engravings, the Society had to wait, however, until much later to obtain a copy of the four-volume double-elephant folio and the octavo edition of *Birds of America*. The former, the Duke of Newcastle copy, came to the Society as the prize gift during its 150th birthday party in 1954. The octavo edition was purchased in 1965. The latter is in original wrappers (most copies were bound) and is far less common than the double-elephant folio. The most well-known Audubon trio was thus complete after 102 years.

One Audubon treasure eludes the Society's collections today. Julius Bien, New York printer and pioneer in chromolithography, in collaboration with Audubon's sons, began producing an American edition of Audubon's *Birds* (Havell's was engraved and printed in England). Production began in 1858, but only 150 plates were completed before the onset of the Civil War stopped the project. The family made little money from the venture and not much is known about the print run. By collecting standards the Bien edition is the scarcest of the Audubon firsts, and the Society still awaits a gift of this edition in order to achieve Audubonic perfection.

During the Bradish presidency the library acquired books and manuscripts at a rapid pace. To keep on the theme of art collecting, scholars of course find paintings themselves as the ultimate objects for study. But documents provide the social and economic details to round out the "picture" or context of artistic creation. In this same period the Society received the archives of the American Art Union, which included 38,000 letters. A prominent group of New Yorkers founded the Union in 1839 for "cultivating artists" and "promoting popular taste." The Union bought paintings from such artists as William Sidney Mount and Thomas Cole and distributed them through a lottery, which cost members an annual fee of five dollars. From 1848 to 1851, a period of sectional strife, the Union published an illustrated periodical, issued engravings to members, and promoted themes of national patriotism. In 1853 it ceased operations and the Society came into possession of its papers. This archive is a most invaluable source for popular culture and taste of the antebellum period.

The Union's distribution of 1,010 works of art in 1849 alone helps us study and understand a multitude of points about the direction and state of artistic taste in the United States. The period was one of intense discussions about creating an "American" culture. Obstacles to achieve this end were abundant given the public's unfamiliarity with art objects and the small number of very wealthy patrons who could afford expensive art. We see at the time heated arguments about the necessity of a democratic culture in order to safeguard political liberty, and thus a particular American culture was created out of this ferment. The danger then, as today, was in the stifling of artistic creativity owing to the mediation of the market. The American Art Union was an important forum in which such important issues were played out, and we learn much about formative artistic endeavors and the pressures put on them through the correspondence and other documentary sources such collections provide. The acquisition of the American Art Union's archive once again illustrates the Society's anticipation of research needs of fledgling scholarly disciplines. The academic study of art history was a long way off, but the Society saved the sources through the housing of such archives.

As the library paved new scholarly roads it didn't neglect the strengths on which it achieved initial fame. During this period of the 1850s and 1860s, the Revolutionary War papers of John Lamb entered the collection, as did a collection of colonial papers of Cadwallader Colden. The latter was lieutenant governor of New York and presided over the colony for fourteen years, until the Revolution. Not only a politician, Colden was a scholar and scientist who wrote the well-known book *The History of the Five Indian Nations Depending on the Province of New York* (1727). The Society of course has more than one first edition of this book. The original draft of DeWitt Clinton's 1816 memorial to the New York State Legislature promoting the Erie Canal, and Oliver Perry's letter to Commodore Isaac Chauncey announcing the victory in the Battle of Lake Erie in 1813, came by way of gift.

One of the Society's most famous manuscripts came in under the Bradish presidency. This was a copy in Clement Clarke Moore's hand of his 1823 poem "A Visit from St. Nicholas" ("The Night before Christmas"). This was a youthful poetic effort by the serious Moore, who only acknowledged authorship in 1837. He was better known during his time as a wealthy writer and philologist who was professor of Greek, Hebrew, and Oriental languages at the General Theological Society. He was also responsible for developing his estate in New York City into the area now known as Chelsea, where his home on Twenty-third Street and Ninth Avenue was located.

The first successful photographic process was the daguerreotype, initially presented to the public in 1839. With the camera one could mechanically record images in minute detail without the mediating influence of the artist or

'Twas the night before Christmas, when all through
  the house
Not a creature was stirring, not even a mouse;
The stockings were hung by the chimney with care,
In hopes that St. Nicholas soon would be there;
The children were nestled all snug in their beds;
While visions of sugar-plums danced in their heads;
And mamma in her 'kerchief, and I in my cap,
Had just settled our brains for a long winter's nap;
When out on the lawn there arose such a clatter,
I sprang from the bed to see what what was the matter.
Away to the window I flew like a flash,
Tore open the shutters and threw up the sash.
The moon, on the breast of the new-fallen snow,
Gave the lustre of mid-day to objects below,
When, what to my wondering eyes should appear,
But a miniature sleigh, and eight tiny rein-deer,
With a little old driver, so lively and quick,
I knew in a moment it must be St. Nick.
More rapid than eagles his coursers they came,
And he whistled, and shouted, and called them by name;
"Now, _Dasher_! now, _Dancer_! now, _Prancer_ and _Vixen_!
On, _Comet_! on, _Cupid_! on, _Donder_ and _Blitzen_!
To the top of the porch! to the top of the wall!
Now dash away! dash away! dash away all!"

As dry leaves that before the wild hurricane fly,
When they meet with an obstacle, mount to the sky;
So up to the house-top the coursers they flew,
With the sleigh full of Toys, and St. Nicholas too.
And then, in a twinkling, I heard on the roof
The prancing and pawing of each little hoof —
As I drew in my head, and was turning around,
Down the chimney St. Nicholas came with a bound.
He was dressed all in fur, from his head to his foot,
And his clothes were all tarnished with ashes and soot;
A bundle of Toys he had flung on his back,
And he look'd like a peddlar just opening his pack.
His eyes — how they twinkled! his dimples how merry!
His cheeks were like roses, his nose like a cherry!
His droll little mouth was drawn up like a bow,
And the beard of his chin was as white as the snow;
The stump of a pipe he held tight in his teeth,
And the smoke it encircled his head like a wreath;
He had a broad face and a little round belly,
That shook, when he laughed, like a bowl full of jelly.
He was chubby and plump, a right jolly old elf,
And I laughed, when I saw him, in spite of myself;
A wink of his eye and a twist of his head,
Soon gave me to know I had nothing to dread;

He spoke not a word, but went straight to his work,
And fill'd all the stockings; then turned with a jerk,
And laying his finger aside of his nose,
And giving a nod, up the chimney he rose;
He sprang to his sleigh, to his team gave a whistle,
And away they all flew like the down of a thistle.
But I heard him exclaim, ere he drove out of sight,
"Happy Christmas to all, and to all a good night."

Clement C. Moore,
1862, March 13th originally written
many years ago.

the creator of the image. In the 1850s, the wet plate method developed, and the public was taken by the accurate representation of the likenesses portrayed. Indeed, photography was acclaimed at the time as being able to portray a higher realm of truth. In 1840 Edgar Allan Poe remarked that the daguerreotype was "infinitely more accurate in its representation than any painting by human hands . . ." Although such writers attempted to link mechanical process to a transcendent level and treat it primarily as an artistic medium, historians would value photography much more for its documentary usage, which seemed unlimited. At first photography was a slow process and used primarily for portraits. But during the Civil War, such photographers as Matthew Brady and Alexander Gardner with their vivid and sometimes gruesome images of war, drove home the full force of this new documentary realism. Visual images dramatically illustrated textual accounts of cataclysmic events. And the Society did not fall behind in its collecting of such resources. True and visionary collectors must anticipate scholarly needs, and the Society was once again up to the task. It is useful here to quote the 1862 _Annual Report of the Committee on Fine Arts_ of the Society:

As it is one of the chief objects of our Society to accumulate materials for the use of future historical students, it is most evident that we should carefully provide for the collection of photographs—not only the likenesses of eminent men and women, but views of streets, houses, landscapes, processions, reviews, battles, and sieges, and indeed almost everything which can be photographed. These should be carefully marked, dated, indexed, classified, and pasted in books. They seem to be small and unimportant by themselves, but when arranged in this way in large numbers, and with proper conveniences of reference, they would undoubtedly form the most valuable auxiliaries to historical inquiry that we could hand down to our successors.

We should note that the author of the report mentioned the importance of having points of access to these materials, such as indexes and classifications. We can forgive the statement on "paste" (although some conservators will never forgive) because pasting in scrapbooks was then an accepted method of storing photographs. The photograph collection would grow dramatically as the Society moved through the next century. Excitingly, many of the photographs that would be given to or purchased by the Society would document this defining period in American history. One especially outstanding example is the rare twenty-eight-volume Meserve collection of *Historical Portraits*. These carte-de-visite-size photographs documented some 8,000 people, arranged by occupation, with a whole volume of Abraham Lincoln photographs. Most of these were originally taken by the Matthew Brady studio. Another is the thirty-one-volume *Photographs of the War of Rebellion*, with several thousand Civil War scenes and portraits. Most were from the negatives of Matthew Brady, E. & H.T. Anthony, and Alexander Gardner. Many other gatherings of photographs documenting American and New York life would enter the collections in the twentieth century.

In 1859 the Society received one of its largest early legacies, a bequest of $10,000 from Seth Grosvenor. These funds propelled the idea of expanding the art collection and opening it up to the public for exhibition.

Mortar "Old Abe"
Photograph by Henry P. Moore,
ca. 1861–1865
Gift of the Military Order of the
Loyal Legion of the United States,
New York Commandery Library

The idea of a free public art museum was taking form and the Society was truly establishing its position in the new national marketplace of ideas.

In 1864 Frederic de Peyster was rewarded for his prodigious fundraising activities by being elected the Society's eleventh president. The next forty years, until the Society's centennial celebration, would be a banner collecting period, but these years would also test its resources in the area of museum and library professionalism. In the initial year of the de Peyster presidency, the Society received its second great collection of paintings, one that was mostly outside its Americana scope, but also one that put it in the forefront of art institutions in the country. This was the collection of Thomas Jefferson Bryan (1803?–1870). Bryan was immensely wealthy and considered one of the first American collectors and connoisseurs of European art. He spent twenty years in Paris, including the periods of the 1830 and 1848 revolutions when artistic spoils came on the market in record numbers and were cheaply acquired. The French novelist Balzac reported that 45,000 paintings were sold yearly during this period. Although Europe may have gone through socially and politically destructive times, they were groundbreaking years for art collectors. Bryan spent much time and money buying from dealers, collectors, and at auction, especially at the famous Artaud de Montor sale of 1851 (mostly paintings from the twelfth to fifteenth centuries).

When he returned to New York he opened the Bryan Gallery of Christian Art and issued a catalogue of 230 paintings in 1853. In 1871 the collection numbered 381 paintings. Bryan's collection had an enormous range and included paintings from the Byzantine period through the twelfth century Europe, Renaissance Italy to contemporary America. American artists included Benjamin West, Gilbert Stuart, Thomas Sully, Charles Willson Peale and his son Rembrandt Peale, and many others. In fact, Bryan bought many of the latter paintings at the sale of the Philadelphia Peale Museum's collections. Bryan's gallery was open to the public at an admission charge of twenty-five cents (political cartoonist Thomas Nast collected the admission charge as a boy). The idea of having Old Masters exhibited in the city caught the fancy of the press which reported that they were "the best and most reliable collection of original works that has ever been accessible to the public in the country" and hoped that Bryan would "establish a permanent and precious shrine . . . to honor, elevate

I Sell the Shadow to Support the Substance.
SOJOURNER TRUTH.

Sojourner Truth carte de visite, 1864

39

and refine the prosperous but perverted instincts of humanity." For various reasons, not least the rise in insurance rates, Bryan closed his gallery and in 1859 lent most of the collection to the Cooper Union. In 1864 he withdrew the art works and offered them to the Society, and the trustees accepted.

The collection came to the Society in 1866 and was deeded in 1867. Sixty additional paintings that Bryan bought during a subsequent trip to Europe were given to the Society after his death in 1870. The Bryan and Reed collections together made the Society the most important art museum in the city until the Metropolitan Museum of Art opened in its present Central Park location in 1880.

The Society's museum had come a long way from its early days as a collector of curiosities and natural history specimens. But this comprehensive approach to art collecting would take its toll on both space and funds. Proper museum collecting is not just in the accumulation and exhibition of treasures; the duty of the museum is to exhibit, store, and properly conserve works of art, as well as to educate the public. It is doubtful that the Society at the time could handle this obligation to posterity. For the most part, well-intentioned amateurs and New York society figures directed the Society at the time and gave little thought to the arrangement, proper access, and conservation of materials. Museum professionalism was in its infancy and the Society was not in the vanguard of this movement. And whether it understood its collecting mission during this period was also questionable, because when a similar collection of European art came along eight years later in 1882, the Society snapped it up with alacrity.

This bequest came from Louis Durr, a member of the Society. Durr (1821–1880) left 158 paintings to the Society, or rather his executors selected the Society for the gift in 1882. Durr immigrated from Germany in 1848 and settled in New York, where he become involved in a gold and silver refining concern. His father was an art dealer, where he probably received some of his art appreciation skills. After making his fortune he bought art on a large scale, perhaps 800 paintings in all. Many of these were sold off after his death to establish the Durr Purchase Fund.

By the time of the gift, 1882, the Metropolitan Museum had opened its building in Central Park and the Society had competition for the acquisition of Old Masters. Because of the Met, the dearth of resources, and future collecting refinements, the Durr bequest was the last large gift of European paintings the Society would see. From this point onward the Society concentrated largely on its primary missions of collecting Americana and particularly art relating to New York City and State. (In 1944 a large deposit, as opposed to a gift, of European paintings would come the Society's way from the New York Public Library, but that is another story.) Many of the European paintings from these collections would be sold off in subsequent years, with some of the proceeds funding additions to the Americana collection. A large number of these out-of-scope paintings, however, went to auction in the 1995–1998 period, during the Society's worst fiscal crisis since the 1820s. But we can safely say that from Luman Reed's large donation of paintings in 1858 through the gifts of the Nineveh marbles, the Abbott Egyptian antiquities, and the Bryan and Durr collections, the New-York Historical Society would represent the best and latest in American artistic taste and collecting.

The catalogue of paintings published in 1915 would attest to the large treasure trove of art in the Society's care. In addition, the Society would be in the vanguard of exhibiting such art to a willing public eager to see the masterpieces of antiquity and the European past. In hindsight it is easy to criticize an institution for this "vacuum cleaner" approach to collecting. But when no other institution existed to preserve such valuable artifacts of the past, it is to the Society's credit that it stepped in to create a museum culture that helped present the fruits of a new American culture to the public, while preserving its European and classical heritage. Few other institutions of the time could equal or even aspire to the Society's achievements on a national scale. The boom of historical societies in the first half of the nineteenth century and beyond were distinctly limited and local. The New-York Historical Society's preeminence in its national role was recognized by people of culture and even the press. Indeed, in 1871 the *New York Times* would comment that the Society "is interesting not only to the man of learning and the savant, but also to every man, woman and child of average intelligence . . ." And in the same year the *Newark Daily Advertiser* would be more effusive in saying, "Probably not a collection of relics, antiquities, records and painting in our common country, or even on the continent of America, can compare with the one in possession of the New-York Historical Society."

While this aggressive and energetic art collecting activity was going on, the research library was continuing to build strength upon strength. In 1867 the Francis Lister Hawks collection was presented to the Society by William Niblo. The Reverend Hawks, preacher, educator, and historian, was a longtime active member of the Society; his most notable work was *Contributions to the Ecclesiastical History of the United States of America* (two volumes; New York, 1836–1839). Although a church historian, his interest covered the entire range of history and he wrote books on *Peruvian Antiquities* and *The Monuments of Egypt*. His wide interests led him to accumulate a large library that would be almost impossible to acquire today. He had approximately two thousand volumes, with about 100 titles of the utmost rarity. When he died in 1866, William Niblo bought the collection en masse and gave it to the Society. Niblo was the proprietor of one of the most popular entertainment establishments in New York at mid-century, Niblo's Garden. It is instructive to look at the interconnection and dynamic here between artistic and cultural patronage and the wealth created through popular culture. Niblo built his "pleasure garden" in 1828 at Broadway and Prince Street. It presented urbane musical and theatrical entertainment along with good food at expensive prices but with elegant service. Although the entertainment was of a higher level than that offered at the Bowery Theatre and other venues of popular entertainment, it was not the classical musical culture of Europe. In fact, New York tried and failed at opera at the same time. Mozart's librettist, Lorenzo Da Ponte, who introduced *Don Giovanni* to New York in the 1820s, raised $150,000 from wealthy New Yorkers to construct an Italian opera house, which opened in 1833. (Some Da Ponte material would end up in the Society's library.) This, the first building in the United States designed and devoted exclusively to opera, was a resounding failure after just two years of operation. Patronage for high culture on the European scale would take some years to develop. But the development of such patronage was in the works with enlightened and philanthropic providers of entertainment (and other services) for the wealthy. New Yorkers did like their entertainment, and those who could afford it went to respectable establishments such as Niblo's. Later on, the Metropolitan Hotel, considered the most magnificent hotel in the city when it opened in 1852, adjoined Niblo's; both were situated on land owned by Stephen Van Rensselaer, a generous patron and member of the Society. We must remember that the Society held its fiftieth anniversary banquet at Niblo's in 1854.

Niblo made his money through such "pleasure palaces" but he also developed an active interest in the historical legacy of the city, and contributed to the cultural tradition that would develop into a richer and more lasting area of aestheticism and historical consciousness. As part of his cultural philanthropic development, he bought Francis Lister Hawks's book collection and gave it to the Society.

These books, immediately named the Hawks-Niblo collection, are a bibliophile's and historian's delight. Not for nothing did R.W.G. Vail, one the twentieth century's bibliographic scholarly giants and director of the Society from 1944 to 1960, state that it "was one of the choicest libraries ever added to the Society's collections."

The Society prepared a catalogue in 1871. The richness of the holdings is staggering and every bookman knowledgeable in Americana would recognize the titles. To cite only some of the high spots, we can write with relish about such books as: Richard Hakluyt, *Virginia Richly Valued* (1609); Thomas Morton, *New English Canaan* (1637); James Rosier, *A True Relation* (1605); Captain John Smith, *A True Relation* (1608); Andre Thevet, *The New Founde World* (1568); Adrian Vanderdonck, *Beschryvinge van Nieuw-Nederlant* (1656); Edward Williams, *Virgo Triumphans* (1650); Edward Winslow, *Hypocrisie Unmasked* (1646), *New England's Salamander* (1647), and *Glorious Progress of the Gospel among the Indians of New England* (1635); and

William Wood, *New England's Prospect* (1635). Perhaps to the average modern reader it is difficult to appreciate the magnitude and value of these books. To take only one example, Richard Hakluyt, we see one of the key players in the period of the exploration, discovery, and colonization of America. Hakluyt was a writer and geographer, most famous for his book *The Principal Navigations, Voiages, Traffiques and Discoueries of the English Nation* (1589; final edition 1598–1600), an indispensable source for the history of geographical discovery and exploration. Hakluyt went on to compose and translate other works, including *Virginia Richly Valued by the description of Florida her next door neighbor*. He produced this tract as the leading advocate of colonizing Virginia. In it, he included a translation of Hernando de Soto's expedition through Florida and the Gulf Coast and suggested the possibility of finding gold in Virginia. Hakluyt is also important in literary history for providing geographical information for Shakespeare and other writers of the Elizabethan period.

In short, these books are a treasure trove of historical sources as well as a bibliophilic paradise. To make sure that these crown jewels of American didn't just stay locked up in a vault, and to illustrate the principle that such books must be both read and seen to be appreciated, the Society frequently had such items on exhibit. For instance, most of the above and other priceless pieces of Americana were on view in the Library Gallery's 1982 exhibition, "A Brief and True Relation: Colonial Americana from the Collections of The New-York Historical Society."

It is a truism that the rich get richer, and when it comes to institutional collection building this is especially true, because strength almost by course of nature builds upon strength. Both donors and researchers see the wisdom of having large related research holdings under one roof. Buckingham Smith, collector of Floridiana and related material, saw the richness of the Society's collection in early Americana and gave it his collection of manuscripts and other items related to Florida. Then, John David Wolfe bought and donated to the Society his large Americana library in 1872. Accompanying the library was a most magnificent artifact loved by all geographers and map collectors alike: the famous Ulpius globe of 1542 which records the discoveries of Giovanni Verrazano in North America. This marvelous globe is on public exhibition at the Society in the Henry Luce Center, after being on display in the library for many years. Entering the collections two years earlier were artist George Catlin's 220 original drawings of American Indians and scenes of Indian life. Catlin, so well known today for his American Indian portfolio, had planned on issuing these drawings in a subscription volume that never saw the light of publication. He had been a longtime member of the Society, and the librarian snapped up the drawings, which entered the collections in 1872.

The Society was fortunate during these years to have a number of wealthy, historically minded members. In the 1870s and 1880s we see such new members as Presidents Rutherford Hayes and James Garfield, and businessmen, collectors, and philanthropists Russell Sage, William K. Vanderbilt, Collis P. Huntington, William W. Astor, and J. P. Morgan. When we see the name of Daniel Parish, Jr. on the membership rolls for the period, we cannot help but smile and think of his future generosity that resulted in the gift of 21,000 slavery-related pamphlets, more than 6,500 manuscripts, and 1,200 Civil War photographs. Parish, who joined the Society in 1882, bought important volumes for the library throughout his life. We do not exaggerate when we say he displayed his generosity almost on a daily basis. He was one of those prescient collectors who bought not just the fashionable but what he believed would be of research importance in the future. In addition to the Civil War and slavery material, he donated many titles on the American West, city directories, and early poetry. He was collecting such material before others even thought of its value. The Society and all research institutions depend on such collectors (and curators and librarians) to anticipate scholarly needs in order to build not just high-spot collections, but ones of depth and breadth. We may compare such collectors as Parish to the seventeenth century English bookseller George Thomason, who systematically collected everything possible on the English Civil War. From the period of the 1640 Long Parliament to the Coronation of Charles II in 1661, Thomason collected approximately 22,000 pamphlets and ephemera, news books, and early newspapers on some of the most burning religious and political issues of the days. In many cases these tracts are the only surviving sources for many of the important events, and his collection is now the main source of much of our knowledge of that period. Following in this tradition is the Society's own Bella Landauer, who amassed one of the largest collections of American advertising ephemera in the country (but more about her later). A man with a vision similar to Parish was Daniel A.P. Murray, who collected African-Americana and bequeathed around 350 pamphlets to the Library of Congress. His collection is rich in post-emancipation material but palls in comparison to the enormity of the Parish collection. The main point, however, is that vision is a necessity for all great collectors, and it is a fortunate and wise institution that has such friends as Parish, Murray, and Landauer dedicated to its mission.

Donors and bequests support the lifeblood of any research institution. This period saw a number of important monetary bequests that strengthened the collections and also pointed toward future expansion. Stephen Whitney Phoenix left his genealogical library of 1,400 volumes to the Society with a fund of $15,000 to make additions to this collection. Such endowments are so important because they provide for future additions, lest the collection becomes a "dead" one.

One of the most exciting bibliophilic events for collectors of Americana and the Society was the great George Brinley sales from 1879 to 1893, where our staff cut their teeth in the fiercely competitive world of the book auction. George Brinley (1817–1885), a wealthy son of a Massachusetts merchant, was one of the few competitors of James Lenox and John Carter Brown in nineteenth century American book collecting. Brinley's collecting took a somewhat different direction from Lenox's and Brown's. Although Brinley was more than willing to pay high prices for books—indeed, he paid $1,000 (a very high sum at the time) for the *Bay Psalm Book*, the first extant book printed in what is now the United States (and one of only eleven known copies), as well as a Gutenberg Bible—he was not beneath scouring discards and other "old" books to find nuggets of Americana. In the latter way he saved an Eliot Indian Bible (the first book printed in an American Indian language and used by John Eliot to convert the natives). In short, he was not the typical high-spot collector of the period. That is not to say that he wouldn't compete with the likes of Lenox for books. A notable example is Brinley's purchase in 1873 from Henry Stevens of a marvelous copy of Captain John Smith's 1624 *History of Virginia*. The Society would have to wait almost a century, until 1971, before receiving its copy of Smith's masterpiece.

By the time Brinley died he had amassed one of the finest collections of Americana in the United States. He did not take the same route as Lenox and

Brown, whose collections would end up in public institutions. (Brown's son would found the John Carter Brown Library in Providence.) Brinley decided that all his books would be sold at public auction. He did believe, however, that many of his books belonged in public institutions, and thus stipulated in his will that a certain amount of money would be given to the New-York Historical Society, the American Antiquarian Society, the Watkinson Library of Hartford, the Historical Society of Pennsylvania, and Yale University, so they could purchase books at his sale. (The Society's own treasurer for a number of years and great American collector Thomas W. Streeter would follow this pattern of combination sale and donation of money to institutions in his instructions for the great Streeter sales of the 1960s.) The five Brinley sales, held between 1879 and 1893, constituted the greatest sale of Americana up to that time. The Society used its money wisely, but not boldly, at the auctions. It bought numerous early and rare New York imprints, almanacs, laws, periodicals, newspapers, and local histories. Besides such items as the 1671 *America* by Arnold Montanus, with its view of New Amsterdam, little of what it bought would bring raves from bibliophiles. Publicity centered on the sale of the *Bay Psalm Book* and the *Gutenberg* (which sold for the unheard of price of $8,000). But the New York material was grist for the research mill, and that was what the Society was about; timid though it may have been at a sale dominated by James Lenox, Yale, and John Carter Brown, it did not lose sight of its mission.

Gifts make an institution great, and one should never lose sight of defining a mission and having interested parties and collectors buy into that mission. Around the time of the first Brinley sale, the Society received one of its most important manuscript collections. In 1880 the Gallatin family gave the library the extensive collection of Albert Gallatin and his descendants. Gallatin, as all those knowledgeable about American history know, was the Swiss native who became Thomas Jefferson's and James Madison's secretary of the treasury, and one of the former's most important advisors. He was to Jefferson what Alexander Hamilton was to Washington in terms of fiscal policy, and was perhaps the only Republican who had the financial knowledge to go head-to-head with

Albert Gallatin
Painting by William H. Powell, 1843
Gift of the artist

Hamilton. Jefferson charged Gallatin with reducing the deficit (how contemporary this all sounds!). Jefferson and Gallatin would actually increase the public debt by over twenty percent, but much of that was owing to the Louisiana Purchase, something that even Hamilton wholly approved. What most of the educated public may not know about Gallatin is that he was the Society's ninth president, from 1843–1849; and under him the Society attracted nearly a thousand new members. Given his government posts—secretary of the treasury, commissioner to Russia (1813), minster to France (1815–1823), and envoy extraordinary to Great Britain (1826–1827), and then president of the Council of New York University, first president of the Ethnological Society, among other offices, his papers are exceedingly valuable for the political, diplomatic, cultural, educational, and economic history of the United States. Any scholar interested in this period of American history must consult this wonderful gathering of materials. Today such a collection of manuscripts would take a fortune to acquire. Rarely do we see such large and comprehensive collections come up for sale today, however, and the ardent collector is usually limited to the acquisition of single items.

If the Gallatin collection did not delight the Society's researchers enough, ten years later the Alexander McDougall papers were added to the holdings. McDougall, a Scottish immigrant, was a privateer during the Seven Years War, amassed a fortune, and later became a merchant in New York. He came to fame during the controversies surrounding the Townshend Acts of 1767 that levied duties on colonial imports of a number of staples. He was a leader of the Sons of Liberty and stirred up revolutionary fervor in New York, first against the Stamp Act and then by leading the defense of the "Liberty Pole" in New York. He presents a splendid example of a rich merchant who had much to lose by defying the British in defense of American rights. In 1769 the anonymous broadside *To the Betrayed Inhabitants of the City and Colony of New York* attacked the aged governor Cadwallader Colden (see above for his collection also in the library) for corruption and urged the colonists to "imitate the noble example of the friends of Liberty in England" who were fighting for their rights. This was a reference to the John Wilkes affair. Wilkes, a member of Parliament, was imprisoned for seditious libel, and became a hero to the radicals in England, whose rallying cry was, "Wilkes and Liberty!" When McDougall was identified as the author of

*Unidentified Woman
(Formerly identified as Edward
Hyde, Lord Cornbury)
Painting by unidentified artist, early
eighteenth century*

To the Betrayed Inhabitants . . . (a copy of course is in the Society's library), he was hailed as the American Wilkes, but was also arrested and tried by Chief Justice Daniel Horsmanden (whose papers are also represented in the Society's collections). McDougall was indicted but never came to trial. During the American Revolution he was a Major General and afterwards with Alexander Hamilton helped organize the Bank of New York, of which he was the first president. The collection given to the Society included over 4,000 military letters and fifteen orderly books. The latter put the Society well on its way to having one of the largest collections of Revolutionary War orderly books in the country. The historian of the American War for Independence well appreciates the importance of military orderly books. They provide records of generals' orders, evidence on daily life in army regiments, orders, work details, disciplinary measures, observations on morale, courts martial, and other areas of military life during the war. Only a few other institutions can compare with the Society in this area of research.

Donors gave more and more collections during this period, including the eighteenth century manuscripts of New York and New Jersey Surveyor-General and Revolutionary War officer William Alexander, as well as 14,000 personal and business papers of the Alexander and Rutherford families. Entering through the library's portal at this time was the 1702 Commission of Lord Cornbury as governor of New York, signed by his cousin Queen Anne. Cornbury was one of the more eccentric, as well as corrupt, governors of early New York. Stories spread of his riding his horse into a tavern, and of him addressing the Assembly wearing female attire. One of the Society's most famous paintings (acquired later) claims to be of Cornbury dressed as a woman (in the fashion of Queen Anne).

Most, if not all, New Yorkers know that real estate is a crucial element in the identity of the city. New Yorkers are also used to the Manhattan traffic jams, which were set in motion well before the automobile was invented. Early nineteenth century city planners knew the value of Manhattan real estate so well that they laid out the streets without allowing for alleys, which would take up valuable land. Thus today, delivery trucks and other service vehicles have to double- and triple-park on city streets, leading to the massive traffic tie-ups to which natives have become accustomed. Also in the early nineteenth century, John Jacob Astor, at that time the city's first millionaire, scoured the city buying up parcels of land. By the 1830s Astor, through his real estate purchases in Manhattan, had become the richest man in the United States. Most of the money spent for land came from his business, the American Fur Company. The Society purchased (for eighty dollars!) the Fur Company records in 1863. The collection of 100 letter books, 15,000 separate letters, and other materials are the primary sources for the pioneer history of the Pacific Northwestern United States and probably the most important business records of the nineteenth century; they are still one of the Society's prized archival collections, and one of the earliest to be preserved on microfilm. This prescient purchase set the stage for the subsequent acquisition of business papers well before economic history became an important scholarly discipline. Astor had sold his interest in the Fur Company by 1830 and put even more money in real estate. At the end of his life he, perhaps apocryphally, mentioned that if he had to do it over again he would do nothing but buy every foot of land in Manhattan. He should see Manhattan real estate prices in the twenty-first century! But we digress.

Land in any city needs "improvements," often meaning buildings. Buildings need architects and engineers. And some of the greatest architects of the nineteenth and twentieth centuries worked in New York. The Society early on began to collect architectural drawing collections from prominent New York firms. The first significant collection of this sort to enter the Society's was that of John McComb, Jr.

John McComb, Jr. was the leading New York architect from 1800 to 1830. He was the architect for the New York City Hall, and the Society's collection contains around 150 drawings for this, his most notable work. A prominent architect later in the century, Charles McKim, called it the "most admirable

Competition drawing for City Hall by John McComb, Jr., 1802 Gift of Daniel Parish, Jr.

building in the city." In 1893 the city attempted to replace McComb's City Hall with another structure. Many prominent New Yorkers answered the call to battle, not least Frederic J. de Peyster, of the family so prominent in Society affairs. They rallied the media, and *Harper's* stated, "The majority of cultivated persons in New York would regard the demolition of City Hall not only as a municipal calamity, but as an act of vandalism." Out of this fight would come the American Scenic and Historic Preservation Society. Other material includes drawings for about 100 church designs and a number of public buildings. McComb was also the architect for Alexander Hamilton's country home, "The Grange." The Grange was also in danger of the wrecking ball but was moved in 1889 to another location in Harlem, now called Hamilton Heights. The McComb collection would lay the groundwork for what would become one of the richest collections of architectural drawings in the city, if not the country.

As both the museum and library collections kept growing, the Second Avenue building became more and more crowded. Early photographs of the museum showed the cluttered look of the walls, with painting upon painting. But as mentioned earlier in this chapter, the concept of the art exhibition was in transition and the crowded walls did not strike the viewer as extraordinary. The Metropolitan Museum of Art was in its infancy and the idea of a focused exhibit was

*Chaise by François Foliot II, 1779
Gift of Anne Cary Morris*

still only evolving. But caring for a large collection that was bursting at the seams was on the minds of Society presidents and trustees in the late nineteenth and early twentieth centuries. Thus, another building campaign gained steam. Under the brief presidency of Eugene Augustus Hoffman in 1901–1902, the Society formed a Building Committee, and by 1902 it had $102,000 in its kitty. Earlier, in the late 1880s, the Society had bought a lot at its present location of Central Park West. Generous donors helped with the purchase price of $286,000. Chief among them with an initial gift of $100,000 was Mrs. Robert L. Stuart, followed by a $25,000 bequest from Robert Schell and a $10,000 gift from Cornelius Vanderbilt. The newspapers enthusiastically supported the new building. The *New York Times* reported on March 9, 1901:

> With a transfer of its home to the lower part of Central Park West there would inevitably come not only the larger rooms which a new building would supply, but renewed activity in the use of books and the attendance upon meetings and lectures. With proper facilities for the display of interesting objects and greater convenience of access, throngs of people would enter its doors where now but few stray in. Indeed, one may contemplate with interesting pleasure the additions which would come to its membership, the historical students who would spend their time in its alcoves, and the crowds of listeners who would gather to hear its lectures . . .
>
> The project certainly ought to possess interest with everyone who knows anything whatever of the splendid history of which this island has been the centre . . . events that have been potent in the life and history of this continent and which should become familiar in the recollections of every American citizen.

The media recognized the national importance of the Society, not only in its collections, but also in its programs, which had lagged for a number of years owing to the state of the Second Avenue building. The move to Central Park West would offer a solution to the institution's problems. Eugene Hoffman died suddenly in 1902, but ground was broken for the building two months following his death. Hoffman's son Samuel Verplanck Hoffman succeeded him in 1903 and presided over the construction of the new Central Park building. In fact, he would dedicate ten years to the building and his family would donate a total of $94,000 for its construction. He also gave over $48,000 for the acquisition of book, manuscript, and art collections, continuing in a stream of generous donors active in maintaining the Society's preeminence in the collecting of Americana. But additional funds were still needed to get the building erected. The librarian (de facto director) at the time, Robert H. Kelby, was able to obtain a gift of $250,000 from the ninety-one-year-old Henry Dexter, in memory of his son Orrando Perry Dexter. As Dexter was president of the American News Company, the media took further notice and sounded the trumpet for the Society's aspirations. A plaque over the door to the auditorium still reads, "The Orrando Perry Dexter Memorial. The Gifts of Henry Dexter Made in Memory of his Son, Orrando Perry Dexter, Have Enabled the New-York Historical Society to Erect this Building."

The collections did not move into the Central Park West building until 1908, but the prospects for the future were very promising and the 1904 Centennial Dinner, held at Delmonico's on Fifth Avenue and Forty-fourth Street, was a happy celebration. Following an eight-course dinner came the traditional toasts. President Samuel Verplanck Hoffman and many others spoke, including an address from librarian Kelby on the growth of the collections and their scholarly value (the latter the Society continually emphasizes). The first hundred years of the Society's existence had seen the acquisition of world famous research and art collections. With the new building in progress, the beginning of the Society's next hundred years looked bright indeed.

Diana of the Tower
Sculpture by Augustus Saint-Gaudens, 1899

Chapter 3
Expansion, Refinement, and Consolidation 1908–1960

The Society achieved its greatest expansion during the presidencies of Samuel Verplanck Hoffman (1903–1912), John Abeel Weekes (1913–1939), George Albert Zabriskie (1939–1947), Fenwick Beekman (1947–1955), and Leroy Kimball (1956–1961).

Because we cannot write biographies of all the Society's presidents and their contributions to the institution in this brief account, let us take as an example the first of this quintet, Samuel Verplanck Hoffman. Hoffman had inherited his father's task (Eugene Hoffman, president, 1901–1902) of erecting a new home for the Society, and he succeeded admirably. His collecting efforts also brought new riches to the Society. All cultural institutions depend for their lifeblood on the magnanimity of their officers and friends for achieving greatness, and Hoffman was an outstanding model of this type of philanthropic executive. Hoffman (1866–1942) received an extensive education, first at the Stevens Institute of Technology, where he graduated with an engineering degree in 1888, and then at Columbia for one year, before spending eight years at the Johns Hopkins University in Baltimore studying astrophysics and astronomy. His business career consisted of managing his father's extensive New York City real estate holdings. He was a pioneering collector of astrolabes, sun dials, and books relating to astronomy. One of Hoffman's most noteworthy gifts to the Society was the astrolabe that Samuel Champlain supposedly used in his explorations of Canada and New York State. Champlain, according to a number of nineteenth century histories, lost his astrolabe after detouring from his route up the Ottawa in order to avoid dangerous rapids. He went through a number of small lakes, and there his astrolabe went astray. In 1867 an adolescent boy found the instrument near Green Lake, Ontario and then sold it to a steamboat captain, who in turn sold it to a merchant in Toronto. Hoffman bought the astrolabe shortly thereafter and the Society received it in the Hoffman bequest. This astrolabe formed the basis for the map issued in the first edition of Champlain's *Les Voyages* in 1613. The map, which shows for the first time the approximate latitude and longitude of the coast of New England and Eastern Canada, came to the Society earlier as a gift from William Cooper in 1813. (The Society, in a "good neighbor" gesture, repatriated the astrolabe to the Canadian Museum of Civilization in 1989.)

Hoffman's tastes were catholic and his generosity crossed collecting media

54

and genres. He was especially instrumental in buying art works at the auction of the E.B. Holden Collection of New York Views in 1910. The Society bought 116 lots, most of them paid for by the president. Some of the more noteworthy works included: Nicholas Calyo's painting of New York from Weehawken; William Rollinson's 1796 original drawing of Government House, with a unique proof of his engraving of same; an original painting of the great fire of New York in 1835; and a wash drawing of New York from Long Island, 1801, perhaps by John Wood. The Society also bought at the same sale a French map of the Siege of Yorktown in 1781, along with a copy of Rochambeau's journal of the siege in the hand of a French army engineer whose own journal was also bought. Another significant painting acquired during the Hoffman years was Francis Guy's *Tontine Coffee House* (ca. 1800).

One of the more scholarly art acquisitions made during the Hoffman presidency was the collection of 378 original wood blocks of the engraver Dr. Alexander Anderson. Acquiring these blocks represents another illustration of the Society's prescient collecting policy with its anticipation of scholarly work on this type of material. Anderson (1775–1870) is known as the "father of American wood engraving." He was a self-taught artist who was making woodcuts for newspapers at the age of twelve. He practiced medicine for a short period in the late eighteenth century and then, after the yellow fever epidemic of 1798, he became a full-time graphic artist, mainly illustrating books and magazines. The collecting of prints or mechanically reproduced art has a long history, but the acquisition of "working" or archival materials of artists is relatively new. Art historians know that the closer one gets to the act of creation the more we can know about the work of art. Therefore, the wood blocks (or the copper plates of the engraver), as well as the successive proofs showing the different states of the prints, are important in documenting each step in the process of creation. It is no accident that museums and libraries try to collect proofs that show the additions or deletions that the artist made to the print. The differences between the initial state and final states can be dramatic. Such archives of printmakers and book artists are in great demand today by art historians and researchers on printing and printmaking techniques; the Society was wise to acquire Anderson's working blocks and make accessible such valuable resources on early American book illustration techniques.

"Join the Army Air Service"
World War I recruitment poster
by Charles Livingston Bull, ca. 1917

The poster collection is one of the striking highlights of the Society's graphic art collections. A number of outstanding examples of poster art came into the institution during the Hoffman presidency. Some of the most sophisticated artistically are those produced in the 1890s by such artists as Edward Penfield and George Wharton Edwards, who produced dazzling art nouveau posters to advertise such magazines as the *Bookman*, the *Century*, *Harper's*, *Scribner's*, and others. The country saw another period of quality artistic endeavors in poster art when America entered World War I. The government produced thousands of posters encouraging the public to support the war effort through enlisting in the armed forces, buying bonds, conserving fuel, and the like. Perhaps the most famous of these World War I posters is Montgomery Flagg's "I Want You" depicting a stern Uncle Sam recruiting America's young and not-so-young to enlist in the armed forces. The Society received over 500 of these war posters after the armistice (including a copy of Flagg's). The poster collection would eventually grow through gift and selective purchases to approximately 5,000, with specimens from the late eighteenth century through Civil War recruiting posters to the present.

World War I, so destructive in many ways, enriched the Society's graphic holdings through an important acquisition. Joseph Pennell (1857–1926) was an American artist and well-known illustrator of American publications who moved to London in 1884. While there he moved in the artistically rich circle that included James McNeill Whistler and George Bernard Shaw. Early on he was an etcher, but during this period took up lithography, publishing the book

Lithography and Lithographers in 1898. Whistler was a great influence on his style, and Pennell's wife Elizabeth wrote the book *The Art of Whistler* (1928). In 1917 Pennell visited war sites and then moved back to New York, where he continued his work and taught courses on etching and illustration. Out of his World War I experience he produced a series of fifty lithographs of war work in America, which the Society acquired during this period. Although the bulk of the Pennell collection went to the Library of Congress, these war lithographs helped bring the print collection into the twentieth century.

Another print collection which bolstered the Society's place in collecting modern prints was the James Boyd collection acquired at the end of the John Abeel Weekes presidency. The Society was always rich in splendid nineteenth century city views, landscapes, and political prints, but the collecting of the twentieth century's more modern prints was not a priority. The Boyd collection laid the foundation for collecting New York prints later on in the century when the Society began actively collecting contemporary prints. In 1935 Boyd began the collection by donating 460 etchings in memory of his wife. The majority of these etchings were views of city life and the collection followed the Society's focus on documenting New York and American life. Boyd added to this collection throughout his life and the holdings represent numerous buildings and other facets of New Yorkiana. But the focus of the Society's collecting was still on the older representations, and it wasn't until the early 1980s that it began broadening the print collection to include later artists, subjects, and print processes. The Boyd and Pennell collections, however, gave the Society a push into and a foundation for twentieth century print collecting.

The Society has a special interest and strength in the sculptures of the American artist John Rogers. Rogers (1829–1904) trained early in his life as a machinist and master mechanic. After the Panic of 1857 he concentrated on drawing and working in clay. In 1863 he began concentrating on sculpting plaster figures and groups, known as "Rogers Groups," that became some of the most popular art objects of

Checkers Up at the Farm
Sculpture by John Rogers, 1877
Gift of Samuel V. Hoffman

57

the nineteenth century. His first major group was the *Checkers Players* (1859), and he then produced a number of gatherings with Civil War themes that appealed to the patriotism of Northerners. He mass-produced his groups, selling them for between ten and fifteen dollars. In all, Rogers produced about 100 different groups and sold about 80,000 pieces, representing themes based on diverse topics that included stories from the writings of Washington Irving, Shakespeare, and other writers (even Goethe). Because of the generosity of President Hoffman, the Society has more than eighty of these groups. Perhaps Rogers is largely forgotten today by the public at large, but at his peak he was one of the most popular American artists of the nineteenth century and the only representative sculptor working in the Realist and genre traditions of that period. In this sense, he was unique and takes his place beside such painters as William Sidney Mount and similar genre artists. The Society's Rogers holdings, achieved through the gifts of Hoffman, make an important contribution to the study of popular taste and art in the nineteenth century.

We must make mention of another art collection received during this period, one that is illustrative of the period's social ferment in the world of New York high society. This was the Peter Marié collection of 284 miniatures of New York's most socially prominent "Four Hundred." The late 1880s were years of intense positioning for places in New York's social "haute monde." The nouveau riche in New York were building larger and larger houses on Fifth Avenue and demanding social access. Perhaps the most intense rivalry was that between the Vanderbilts and the Astors. Caroline (Mrs. William) Astor presided over society's inner circle and Ward McAllister famously made the pronouncement that the most elite of New York's social world were the "Four Hundred" that could be accommodated in Mrs. Astor's ballroom. But in a society that didn't strictly depend on a blood lineage aristocracy, challenges to the group were constant. Mrs. Astor met her match in Mrs. Vanderbilt. In 1883 Alva Vanderbilt gave a large ball in her Fifty-second Street mansion and left Mrs. Astor off the invitation list until the latter was "properly introduced." Mrs. Astor surrendered by sending Mrs. Vanderbilt her calling card; the Vanderbilts entered proper society and through this act Astor was able to retain her hold on the inner circle for another decade. (In 1951 the Society would feature an exhibit on the Vanderbilt Ball.) In 1892 McAllister issued a list of names of the Four

Hundred (actually only 273 names) to the *New York Times*. High society, however, was fluid, and more wealth produced additional inductees into the inner circle. One historian called it a social bureaucracy by this time, with thousands achieving the much envied grade. It was becoming difficult for the social-information-starved to keep track of who was who in the New York social whirl. One just had to keep up, but how was this to be done? Entrepreneurs always come along to help out the curious, and to make a little money on the way. Louis Keller thus began publishing the *Social Register* in 1887, which listed nearly two thousand socially prominent New Yorkers, with their names, addresses, birth dates, colleges, and other pertinent information. The lists remained open and the dynamic status climb certainly helped the city's economy. The *Register*, which began as a tool of snobbism, became a unique source for New York social history, and the Society naturally has a long run of this peerless directory for the use of historians and the curious alike. Artist Peter Marié's portraits (originally bequeathed to and turned down by the Metropolitan Museum of Art) give historians splendid documentary evidence of those days of Astor society dominance when it was possible for one doyenne to ordain the chosen few.

Although the Astor-Vanderbilt feud was the most prominent social war of the period, another battle that took its toll on this not-so-cozy social world was the opera war that pitted the old New York society and its own Academy of Music against the new social "upstarts." After Commodore William H. Vanderbilt was snubbed by the Academy when he couldn't buy an opera box for the whopping sum of $30,000 in 1880, he gathered a formidable army composed of Morgans, Rockefellers, Whitneys, Goelets, and others to found the Metropolitan Opera and build a grand new opera house on Broadway and Thirty-ninth Street. The new house opened with a performance of Gounod's *Faust* in 1883. The Met was so successful that the Academy of Music couldn't compete and folded some few years later. The New-York Historical Society's own collections reflect much of this event, and in 1983 it would stage an exhibition celebrating the Met's centennial. The Society found itself in a similar situation some decades later when it would experience its own turmoil among its members as a coup was launched against its leadership. This was "Mrs. Van Rensselaer's War."

During World War I, the Society experienced a lull in its activities and attendance. Few salaried staff were in attendance, with only three professionals to run the library and museum. Since attendance at business meetings was sparse, members of the Executive Committee of the Society attempted to place the power of running the institution in their own hands. Their successful proposal was that the Board could control all activities of the Society for three years without consulting the membership. Here, in 1916, Mrs. John King Van Rensselaer stepped in with very serious charges against the management, led by Samuel Hoffman's successor as president, the prominent New York lawyer John Abeel Weekes. The *New York Times* reported on December 9, 1919 that Mrs. Van Rensselaer charged that the Society "was in the rear of organizations of its kind, instead of being in the forefront, that she was ashamed of it, that she had not heard one new or advanced scientific thought expressed at its meeting in three years, that few attended the meetings because they were 'uninteresting and dull' and that 'instead of an imposing edifice filled with treasures from old New York, what do we find? Only a deformed monstrosity filled with curiosities, ill-arranged and badly assorted.'"

Although this statement was exaggerated for political impact, it is true that the Society at the time was not in the vanguard of museum activities in the country. Much of the most important work at the time centered on the research library, and even there, arrangement, access, conservation, and exhibitions did not keep up with accumulation of materials. Mrs. Van Rensselaer had met and discussed these charges with other dissidents for some years before she decided to contest the election of 1920. Mrs. Van Rensselaer had been keeping tabs on the Society for about five years. Apparently she despised the librarian Robert Kelby and his staff, and thought the latter had usurped the managing functions of the volunteer officers. She charged that "the actual management of the Society has fallen into the hands of the subordinate officers and it is probably not venturing too much to say that many of the members of the Executive Committee have little knowledge of the Society's affairs and take little active interest in the details of its operations." In addition, she charged that the Society was "either dead or moribund." Because of the years she spent visiting the Society and writing down what she considered its deficiencies, she did not just pull these accusations out of her rather formidable hat.

Mrs. Van Rensselaer and her supporters presented a rival ticket for the 1920 election, an insurgency unheard of in the Society's 116-year existence. We cannot deduce from the reports, either internal or from the media, that the pedigree of the two rival slates of officers differed in any marked degree. This was a war fought mostly among old New Yorkers, and not a battle between the anciens et modernes such as the *Social Register* and opera wars (although we see a mixture and crossing of party/social lines in all of these encounters). What is clearly significant, however, in the uprising is what the *Times* reported and what was apparently not picked up on by other historians of the Society: "Though both tickets involve some changes from the present officership . . . the new ticket proposes alone and for the first time to give women the privilege of holding office." This proposal was revolutionary indeed and probably brought fear into the most stalwart Society (and society) members and supporters. The so-called "conservative" faction countered in a letter of its own stating that the insurgents' "attack is not only untrue, but in every way discreditable to those who offer it, while the long and admirable service of its subordinate officers [the professionals—we are still dealing with benevolent philanthropical amateurs here] does not justify any statement reflecting on their fidelity and usefulness." The letter went on to say that the Society effected improvements in the Egyptian collections and the cataloguing of its manuscript collections, with a stress on its strong financial condition. We hear only silence on the issue of women officers. The insurgents nominated for their slate Mrs. Edward H. Harriman for first vice president and Mrs. Francis Bishop for domestic secretary.

The big meeting occurred on January 6, 1920 and John Abeel Weekes and the "regulars" beat back the insurgents 512 to 79 in this first contested election in the Society's history. We must not take the idea of women officers lightly during this period of suffragist ferment. After more than sixty years of organized struggle dating from the Seneca Falls conference of 1848, women were just getting their voting rights. They received the franchise in New York in 1917 and three years later nationally through the ratification of the Nineteenth Amendment. In the sense of battling for women's rights, Mrs. Van Rensselaer was a revolutionary, although she would have shuddered at the mention of the word. Women took their rightful place in the Society's leadership later on, but they would have to wait until the 1967 when Mrs. John Kean took a seat on the

Board of Trustees (created in 1937 as successor to the Executive Committee), and 1988 for a woman to become director. Mrs. Van Rensselaer lost this battle but that was by no means the end of her. She first wrote a scathing twelve-page letter to the Society in which she repeated many of her charges. She then went off and organized the Society for Patriotic New Yorkers with its own museum at Gracie Mansion. The top class of membership (by invitation only) was restricted to those who had ancestors resident in the state before 1776. In 1923 the newly formed Museum of the City of New York took over the Gracie Mansion site and spent four years restoring it before opening as a museum in 1927. Later on the Museum moved to its present site on upper Fifth Avenue. This would not be the end of the story of the secession in the Society, because when it had its serious financial crisis, beginning in the 1980s, talks would begin about the two institutions joining forces and combining into one historical museum. These attempts would all eventually fail, the last time in the Society's bicentennial year of 2004.

The library received one of its finest gifts during this period. The five-thousand-volume private library of Rufus King, Charles Ray King, and John Alsop King came in shortly before the opening of the Central Park West building. Rufus King was, of course, one of the Framers of the Constitution, having represented Massachusetts at the Constitutional Convention in 1787, and was by all accounts one of the two authors (with James Wilson) of the Constitution's state ratification process, which almost assured the document's passage. Shortly after his work was done in Philadelphia, he entered New York politics and in 1789 was one of New York's first senators. In 1804 and 1808 he ran unsuccessfully for vice president of the United States on the Federalist ticket, and in 1816 for president. His son John Alsop King was governor of New York, and his grandson became the Society's eighteenth president. Having such friends is always a bonus for a cultural institution, and the King family showed their generosity through the donation of their library of incomparable significance to anyone researching the early discovery and colonization period of America. Included were such rarities as Daniel Denton's *A Brief Description of New York* (London, 1670), which was the first account of New York in English, and Charles Wolley's *A Two Years Journal in New York [1678–1680]* (London, 1701), one of only a half-dozen known copies.

One of the highlights of this period was the acquisition of the twenty-eight-volume manuscript diary of Philip Hone. We have mentioned Hone above, especially in the context of early nineteenth century art collecting. Hone's reputation and value to historians, however, reside in his detailed diary of city life from 1826 until 1851. Hone (1780–1851) served as mayor of New York in 1825 and presided over the opening of the Erie Canal, as well as the New York reception for the triumphal return visit of the Marquis de Lafayette. Hone's diary is probably the primary source of New York social and political life from the view of the social elite during the first half of the nineteenth century and is only rivaled by the George Templeton Strong diary, which the Society would also acquire some years later. Hone's manuscript is best known in the edited, but not complete, version of historian Allan Nevins. Another manuscript of great historical significance that entered the library collections at this time was the orderly book that gives the only official record of Nathan Hale's execution as a spy by the British.

The Society acquired one of the most outstanding manuscripts in the United States during Hoffman's presidency. This was the so-called Edwin Smith Surgical Papyrus that was added to the Egyptian collections. This papyrus from the seventeenth century B.C. is one of the oldest extant medical manuscripts in the world. The papyrus consists of a systematic arrangement of forty-eight cases (rather than the usual medical recipes found in such papyri), beginning with the injuries of the head and proceeding downward throughout the body. It apparently is a partial copy of an older manuscript from 3000–2500 B.C. The Society, in its efforts to stay true to its original collecting mission, deposited the papyrus in the New York Academy of Medicine in 1948 where it became the prize of the collection. This transfer is a splendid example of philanthropy in which one institution realizes the logic of and value to researchers of having materials housed in a repository whose collections facilitate their study.

The abundance of material the Society collected for over a century proved too much for even the new building, and John Abeel Weekes, now firmly in control after the Van Rensselaer insurgency, initiated a fundraising campaign to build wings on the Central Park West building. Weekes, stating that the Society "owned the largest permanent exhibition of art in the country," put on display

Armchair
Artist unknown, 1785–1789
Gift of Edmund B. Southwick

a dazzling array of paintings to entice the public to support the proper exhibition of materials that only new space could afford. He also stated that "our building is absolutely full—it has become a mere storehouse where the treasures are preserved." He went on to report that the collection held 1,045 paintings, 250,000 books, 5,000 volumes of newspapers, as well as large museum and archival collections.

Exhibitions also played a significant part in the Society's campaign. In 1920 the *New York Times* raved about a display of engravings, prints, posters, and broadsides featuring George Washington and Abraham Lincoln. The *Times* stated, "There has of late been such a great revival of interest in these two patriots that the exhibition is meeting with popular favor." History was back! Later in the year, the *Times* would write about the array of rare books the Society would put out in commemoration of the tercentennial of the Pilgrims landing in New England on December 21, 1620. Many of the seventeenth century rarities mentioned above would be on exhibition and the newspaper would exclaim that the books and manuscripts were worth "between $400 and $5,000 each." Value always counts in the public's eye.

The Egyptian collections would continue their hold on the media's attention. In 1923 the Society would put on display a number of objects from its 3,000-plus Egyptian holdings. The *Times* took special notice of a splendid ring from the Egyptian pharaoh Tutankhamen and a bas-relief from the same dynasty. The newspaper discussed how the American contribution to knowledge about ancient Egypt only dated back to the beginning of the twentieth century and that the Abbott collection was one of the country's key holdings for the advancement of research into this famous Egyptian dynasty. This article was good publicity indeed for the Society because we must remember that in 1923 Tutankhamen was all the rage after archeologist Howard Carter's discovery of the pharaoh's tomb in November 1922.

Historical archeology of New York also had a place in the Society's activities during the years of these five presidents. For example, the Field Exploration Committee worked assiduously under William Louis Carver and Reginald Pelham Bolton for twenty years and explored numerous New York sites, including Revolutionary War sites in Manhattan, the Bronx, and Staten Island, as well as colonial dwellings such as the site of an abandoned homestead on the dividing line between Riverdale and Spuyten Duyvil. Bolton and Carver published their findings, first in articles, and then in the influential book *History Written with Pick and Shovel*, one of the first such works on the subject.

The *Quarterly Bulletin* of the Society began publishing in 1917 and became the leading journal for disseminating scholarly articles on New York for over sixty years until its demise in 1980 because of a fiscal crisis. (We are pleased to note that the journal has been revived in recent years.) The Society was obviously not "dead and moribund" as the Van Rensselaer faction charged. In fact, the institution was on the move. Until the Weekes presidency, the Society had only two professional staff, the librarian and assistant librarian. In 1917 five professionals were hired, with more to come.

Also in 1917 the Society brought in three consultants to do what we would call today a program or management review, studying all the operations of the institution. Three better scholars and professionals could not be found at the time: Worthington C. Ford of the Massachusetts Historical Society, John W. Jordan of the Pennsylvania Historical Society, and Clarence Brigham of the American Antiquarian Society. All had doctorates and were prominent librarians and bookmen. We should note the "bookmen" attributes of these gentlemen. They were concerned with the running of historical research institutions, not museums. And that is not unusual given that the museum profession was relatively new and did not as yet produce the experienced consultants so readily available in the book field. In fact, it was not until the presidency of Robert G. Goelet (1971–1987) that the Society would have a "museum" person in charge. Brigham, in his official report remarked :

If certain work has not been done, if certain publications have not been compiled, if certain kinds of assistance have not been furnished, it is because the officers have not been provided with the necessary means to fulfil these obligations. And this has always been the besetting sin of the Society from the beginning. How it has accomplished so much with so little has always been a source of wonder to those most familiar with its working. It seems to me that in a community which boasts of the greatest wealth of any city on the continent there should be little trouble in persuading the possessors of riches to support adequately an institution which has done so much, and could do so much more, to give New York its proper place in the history of the nation.

Brigham had put his finger on the Society's perennial problem. Great research institutions need the financial support of a wide public, and the Society always had difficulties in attracting this support. Even at this time, in 1917, the collections far surpassed most other similar institutions and they still lead the way in the twenty-first century. Scholars, by their very nature, do not usually have the financial wherewithal to give substantial support. The responsibility is on the concerned public to make their cities great by making their cultural institutions great.

The Society formed its own committee to study the physical plant and the museum and art collections. The committee authorized new cases for the Egyptian collections, the cleaning of paintings, and for the cataloguing of books and manuscripts. Although the committee and officers complained bitterly of Mrs. Van Rensselaer's "unjust" criticisms, she surely was the source or motivation to take a fresh look at operations. All private and public institutions need such occasional prodding or shaking up lest they become too complacent and lax in their responsibilities to posterity. And Mrs. Van Rensselaer certainly prodded.

After the Van Rensselaer revolt the Society embarked on an all-out campaign to expand the Central Park West building to accommodate the growing collections. A new age was beginning. The most outstanding representative of the outgoing generation, however, was librarian Robert Kelby, who resigned in 1921 after fifty-three years of service and presiding over a period of great growth of the collections. Assistant librarian Alexander J. Wall succeeded him and would remain the librarian until 1937 when his title was changed to director. (Until 1937 the librarian was always the de facto director or professional in charge of the operations of the Society.) Under Wall's leadership the Society became perhaps the leading institution of the time for the study of American history.

The need for new space was critical not long after the opening of the new building, so fundraising for the addition of wings began in earnest with a gift of $20,000 in 1922 by the Frenchman Duc de Loubat. Loubat had been a member of the Society for over fifty years when the *New York Times* reported his generous gift on July 2, 1922. The year before he had given $5,000 to mark his fiftieth year as a Society member. With these and a few other gifts, the Society had enough money to draw up plans for the expansion and also to buy the buildings adjoining the Society for its future course. It still didn't have, however, the $1.5 million needed to complete the job. To be sure, other donations and bequests came in, including $54,000 from George W. Van Slyck, more than $50,000 from Ellen King, and $60,000 from a number of others. The James Wilbur bequest of $100,000 didn't help the building effort, but was of particular significance for the library. The Society established an endowment for the purchase of books and manuscripts. One need only peruse the annual reports for the remainder of the twentieth century to see the good to which the Wilbur Fund was put in the service of acquiring rare Americana.

The great stroke of fortune for the Society's future came in the form of the Thompson bequest. On February 25, 1920, the *New York Times* reported that a settlement had been made over the litigation of the will of Charles G. Thompson, who died on December 8, 1919. Thompson left much of his money to six institutions, one of which was the New-York Historical Society. Thompson was a trustee of the New York Life Insurance and Trust Company, founded by his father, David. The latter died in 1907 and left his fortune to his three children—David, Elizabeth, and Mary. And there the affair gets complicated because each heir drew identical wills which mainly left life interests to each other, with the residuary estate of the survivor going to the six institutions. The last sibling, Mary, died in 1935 at the age of ninety-one. All three were descended through their mother from Lyon Gardiner, the founder of the seventeenth century manor of Gardiner's Island, east of Long Island. It was in anticipation of receiving this money that the Society made plans for additions to its building. By the time the bequest came in, between 1935 and 1942, the Society reaped a windfall of $4,633,915.62, a princely sum at the time.

With this money the Society was able to authorize the completion of the Central Park site, as well as build up the endowment. In preparation for the additions, Society treasurer at the time, George Zabriskie (and president, 1939–1947), took librarian Alexander Wall on a tour of Europe to study museum design and construction. With the latest ideas in museum lighting and design as models, the new wings to the building were completed in 1938. In addition to the wings, the building was renovated and fifteen levels of book stacks were added at the rear of the building. The official opening took place on April 1, 1939, and for the first time the Society had adequate exhibition galleries, workspace, and storage. This truly began a new era for the Society in all areas of its operations. For this first time an aggressive art exhibition schedule could be maintained. But before that function could actuate, the Society needed more professional staff.

White Swallow clipper ship card
Printed by Nesbitt and Co. [n.d.]
Clipper Ship Card Collection

The newly acquired endowment allowed the Society to build up its specialist staff. In 1937, with Alexander Wall as director, the Society hired a librarian, a bibliographer, a manuscripts curator, a number of museum curators, conservators, and others. In 1938 the Society had forty-eight employees, up from the seven professionals on board in 1917. More were to come until the count totaled seventy-five staff by the 150th anniversary in 1954. Library reading room space doubled, a manuscripts room was added, and other special collections rooms were opened. The new professionalism, the size of the building, and the added responsibilities of the entire organization prompted the Executive Committee to change its name to the Board of Trustees, following a model in place at the Metropolitan Museum of Art and the Society's Central Park West neighbor, the American Museum of Natural History.

In 1939 the Society reached its maximum size on Central Park West. It would have other storage facilities for its vast newspaper, art, and other collections, though the main building, because of New York City landmark regulations, would remain as it is. But the space provided by the new wings made it all the more active in the building of its collections. One of the most unique and valuable of these collection to researchers and museum-goers alike was the Landauer collection, which finally had a room of its own. It was also one of the largest collections in the building and the largest of its kind in America.

68

The Landauer Collection of Business and Advertising Ephemera is arguably the best such collection in the United States. (A similar, but smaller collection is at the Smithsonian Institution in Washington, D.C.) Bella Landauer (1884–1960) began collecting ephemera soon after World War I when she was advised, for health reasons, to become active in a hobby. And she did so with a gusto rarely seen among even the most

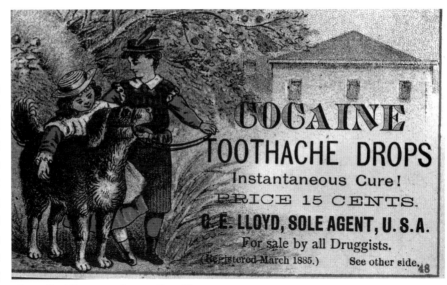

Cocaine Toothache Drops
Advertising trade card, ca. 1885
Bella C. Landauer Collection

avid collectors. She started collecting what she called "scraps of paper" and kept adding to them up until her death. She made her first donation to the Society in 1926 and the library made space for much of the collection in the Landauer Room in the newly renovated and expanded building. Over her lifetime she gathered a collection of approximately one million items that included bookplates, trade cards, commercial fans and paperweights, menus, valentines, club membership booklets, invitations and announcements of social events, telegrams, lottery tickets, and poster art. The smallest item in the collection is Tom Thumb's (of Barnum Circus fame) miniature calling card. She was an indefatigable collector and we always think of the perhaps apocryphal story of Mrs. Landauer alighting from a cab in front of the Society, and in front of astonished onlookers, at 9:00 a.m, clutching several empty whiskey bottles. She was going to her office to soak the labels off and add them to her collection. Mrs. Landauer spent many hours in the Society arranging these pieces in large folio scrapbooks, usually by the product or service category.

The largest segment of her collection is representative material from widely advertised products such as clothing, patent medicines, dry goods, food and beverages, theatrical enterprises, tobacco items, and transportation. A large sheet music collection features such subjects as New York City events, dances, and women's suffrage themes. Cocaine-based medical remedies are popular subjects for researchers, and warriors on illegal drugs would get apoplectic seeing the large and popular chromolithographed poster advertising cocaine as a cure for male baldness. Be that as it may, serious business and advertising his-

Perroquet's speakeasy card [n.d.]
Bella C. Landauer Collection

torians from all over the world make the pilgrimage to the Landauer collection to study this unique gathering of valuable and colorful material.

The Society has continually added to this collection to the present day. For instance, a marvelous collection of unused and proof cigar box labels was given to the Society in the 1980s by donor Sidney Voice. The Society's speakeasy cards are wonderful additions to this collection and of course provide colorful examples of the failure of yet another war on an illegal (at the time) substance. These cards certainly enrich any study of the 1920s in America. Such material gives the historian a remarkable look at popular culture in all its artistic manifestations. Bella Landauer not only collected hundreds of thousands of items, but she also documented the collecting of ephemera. Her correspondence and published writings contribute to the history of both advertising and collecting in this fascinating area. Mrs. Landauer also followed the dictum we have stated before, that strength builds on strength. She collected and donated not only advertising and business ephemera, but material in other areas that she gave to institutions with similar materials and research interests. For example, her collection of European trade cards, French wine labels, and Japanese matchbook covers went to the Metropolitan Museum of Art, and her aeronautical pictures went to the National Air and Space Museum and the Library of Congress. We must count Bella Landauer as one of the Society's most loyal collecting friends and donors.

More and more collections came in during this exciting period. In the years extending from the Hoffman presidency to the sesquicentennial in 1954, the Society became one of the leading centers for the study of architecture. We have already mentioned the John McComb collection. Significant records of architectural firms followed the New York City Hall architect's holdings into the Society's research collections. In all, the architectural collections number about 130,000 pieces, including drawings, blueprints, photographs, and other materials. In such a short survey as this we cannot mention all the treasures, but the collection is so rich for the study of New York and American architecture, given the prominence of the firms, that we would be remiss in not mentioning the most important. For example, the Alexander J. Davis Architectural Drawing Collection found a home at the Society. Davis (1803–1892) was one of the most innovative and influential architects of the mid-years of the nineteenth century. Davis designed many Gothic Revival, Italianate, and bracketed-style residences in the Hudson River area, but his work spreads from Maine to North Carolina, with his earliest successes located in Indiana. (He was responsible for the state capitol in collaboration with architect Ithiel Town.) He designed the patent office in Washington, D.C., the University of Michigan, and the Virginia Military Institute. The collection presently numbers approximately 800 architectural drawings with a heavy New York representation. Samuel Hoffman donated the bulk of the collection in 1927.

In 1953 the Society received the gift of the John B. Snook Architectural Record Collection. Snook (1815–1901) was best known for his designs for the Grand Central depot and the first elaborate department store, that of Alexander B. Stewart on Broadway in lower Manhattan. The collection includes approximately 2,500 drawings and numerous contract books, blueprints, account books, and other business papers.

Near the end of this period, Edward E. Post donated his famous grandfather George B. Post's architectural record collection of approximately 8,600 drawings, 200 watercolor renderings, as well as numerous photographs, manuscript letters, ledgers, employment records, and publications. Post (1837–1913), after studying civil engineering, studied architecture with Richard M. Hunt, and in 1860 partnered with Charles D. Gambrill. In 1868 Post had his own firm and designed many commercial buildings. His work includes the New York Cotton Exchange, the New York Produce Exchange, the New York Stock Exchange, the College of the City of New York, the Pulitzer Building, the Wisconsin State Capitol, and the residences of Cornelius Vanderbilt and Collis P. Huntington. Post is most noted for his role in developing the modern office building and the modern skyscraper. Unfortunately, many of his buildings didn't survive America's constant urban rebuilding. The collection includes most of the surviving records of his early partnership with Gambrill, as well as those of his own firm (to 1905) and that of Post and Sons (after 1905). His work on the

Equitable Life Assurance Society's first headquarters building in New York is considered the city's first skyscraper. Fire destroyed the building in 1912.

In 1950 Stanford White's son, Lawrence Grant White, donated a voluminous collection of the papers of the McKim, Mead, and White architectural firm. Architects Charles Follen McKim (1847–1909), William Rutherford Mead (1846–1928), and Stanford White (1853–1906) were probably the most prominent architects of the Gilded Age; in fact, they were called the "most dazzling architect triumvirate" in America. McKim was the original leader. He attended Harvard and studied at the Ecole des Beaux-Arts in Paris, and then apprenticed in New York with architect Henry Hobson Richardson for two years. Mead worked with Russell Sturgis, then spent two years in Florence before joining McKim. The two partnered with McKim's brother-in-law William Bigelow until the partnership disbanded after Annie Bigelow abandoned McKim in 1878. Stanford White became a nineteen-year-old apprentice of the above-mentioned H.H. Richardson in 1872. In 1878 he left Richardson and went to Europe, where he worked with the sculptor Augustus Saint-Gaudens for fifteen month before returning to New York and teaming up with McKim and Mead. White's fame as an architect was almost eclipsed by his notoriety as a playboy and his violent, sensational death on the rooftop theatre of Madison Square Garden, a building of his own design. Harry K. Thaw, an unbalanced thirty-seven-year-old Pittsburgh millionaire, was married to the former "Gibson Girl" Evelyn Nesbit. Nesbit was a mistress of White when she was sixteen years old and Thaw knew of this past relationship. On June 25, 1906 Thaw walked over to White's table and pumped three bullets into him. Thus ended the partnership. Readers familiar with the novel and movie *Ragtime* will

Elevation of Washington Square Arch by McKim, Mead, and White, ca. 1889
Gift of Lawrence Grant White

recognize the story. Most important for this tale, however, is the work the firm designed and completed, and its significance for New York's architectural history. The three architects brought different strengths to the partnership: McKim was a designer with a deep understanding of decorative arts and early American style who also had the connections and client list to keep the firm in commissions; White was an artist who created elegant and original buildings; Mead ran the office and made sure the others "didn't [make] damn fools of themselves." Together they towered over the architectural world for more than twenty-five years. Their buildings included Madison Square Garden, the Villard Houses, the Pierpont Morgan Library, Brooklyn's Prospect Park entrances, the Boston Public Library, the Rhode Island State Capitol, and many other buildings. The Society's archive contains approximately 48,000 architectural drawings, 1,500 photographs, 650 boxes of correspondence, and numerous business ledgers, account books, and the like. The Society's Manuscript Department holds the Stanford White family letters.

The final architectural gift we will mention is the large and valuable Cass Gilbert collection, given by the architect's children Cass Gilbert, Jr. and Emily Gilbert. Gilbert (1859–1934) received his education at the Massachusetts Institute of Technology, where he won several awards for his architectural drawings. After graduation he spent some time traveling in Europe where he hoped to work in a London architectural firm. When that didn't happen he came back to America and went to work for McKim, Mead, and White in 1882. In 1885 he started an architectural firm with James Knox Taylor and then branched out on his own in 1892. Gilbert became one of the best known architects in the country because of his high-profile buildings which include his most famous one, the Woolworth Building (designated the "cathedral of commerce") in New York (completed in 1913), the United States Custom House in New York, and the Supreme Court Building in Washington, D.C. The onset of the Modernist movement in the 1920s eclipsed some of Gilbert's work, but late twentieth century historians have recently recognized his outstanding contribution to American architecture. The collection includes approximately 63,000 architectural drawings, 245 cubic feet of incoming correspondence, 469 volumes of outgoing correspondence, and a large cache of business records and other materials. The Gilbert collection is a goldmine for researchers in the art and

Woolworth Building
Architectural drawing by Thomas R. Johnson, 1910
Gift of Cass Gilbert, Jr. and Emily Gilbert

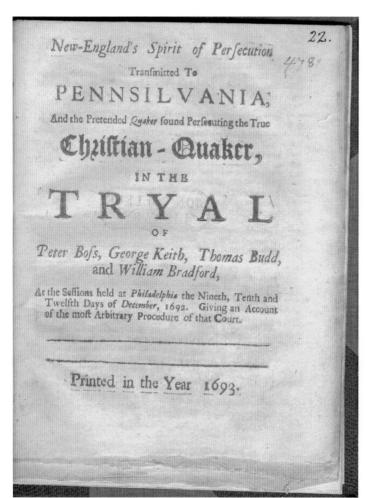

New-England's Spirit of Persecution Transmitted to Pennsylvania . . .
(n.p.: William Bradford, 1693)
Arguably the first book printed in New York

business of building. The Society's architectural collections, along with those of the Avery Architectural Library of Columbia University, make the upper West Side of Manhattan a mecca for historians of architecture of America, and especially of New York.

The years after the opening of the new building brought a flurry of activity in the acquisition of rare and valuable books. For those who wonder just what a "rare" book is, we always say that it has to be scarce, be important in content, and someone has to want it. It is not rare if nobody desires to possess the object. The market always puts the monetary value on significant material. The Society has an abundance of such items, seldom bought for the iconic status, but always purchased for the research value added for the community of scholars.

William Bradford, New York's first printer, comes to mind when we think of rarity in a New York context. Not only are his books of primary importance for New York history in general, but also for the history of printing in America. The Society always bought his imprints when they came on the market and these years saw the acquisition of his *Good Order Established in Pennsilvania & New Jersey* (1685) by Thomas Budd; *News of a Trumpet Sounding in the Wilderness* (1697); *Gospel Order Revived* (1700); the only known perfect copy in America of *An Account of the Illegal Prosecution and Tryal of Col. Nicholas Bayard, in the Province of New-York, for Supposed High Treason* (1702); and one of two known copies of *A Narrative of the Treatment Col. Bayard Received* (1702). The subject of the latter two publications, Nicholas Bayard, played a prominent role in New York history. Bayard's 1693 book on Governor Benjamin Fletcher was one of the first books printed in New York. Bayard was prominent in opposing and crushing the rebellion in New York led by Jacob Leisler after England's Glorious Revolution of 1688. Bayard, after being imprisoned by the Leislerians, supposedly persuaded Governor Sloughter while the latter was drunk to sign Leisler's death warrant the following year. Leisler was executed in 1691. Leislerians took back the provincial government some years later and Bayard himself was tried and convicted of treason in 1702. Bayard, unlike Leisler, received a pardon.

Bradford's publications were the official records sent by Governor Cornbury to Queen Anne. Accompanying the Bradford imprints on Bayard coming into the Society at the time was the 1703 London publication, *An Account of the Commitment, Arraignment, Tryal and Condemnation of Nicholas Bayard, Esq.; for High Treason*. If having these rare imprints on Bayard was not enough for any research library, the Society also received 600 eighteenth century manuscripts relating to this important New York official. Other Bradford imprints the library acquired were his 1704 *A Little Olive Leaf* and the only known copy of his *A Plat-Form of Church Discipline* of 1711. A rarity of Americana of great religious significance came to the Society at this time: the first edition (1830) of *The Book of Mormon*, with the very scarce four-page table of references at the end. We must remember also that the founder of Mormonism, Joseph Smith, started his religious journey in Palmyra, in upstate New York. So many rare books and newspapers came into the library's collections during this half-century that we can only mention a few. But books such as the Bradford imprints reflect the quality of the library's holdings and we can compare these publications to the earliest European books in order to gauge the quality of the Society's collection. And it is not found wanting. The Society continued to purchase and receive by gift other Bradford books, but one of the most spectacular finds comes later in this story.

To mention only two more book collections coming in during these years of plenty, let us look first at the Charles M. Wetzel collection on American fishing. Numbering over 1,500 pieces, it is one of the finest collections of its kind in an American institution, and the gift of Otto Kienbusch. Prominent New York rare book dealer Lathrop G. Harper gave the Society over 6,000 items in his Spanish-American War collection. Perhaps more important in many ways is the Lathrop G. Harper bequest. Coming to the Society in 1958, $200,000 established the Lathrop Colgate Harper, Litt.D. Fund, and $50,000 the Lathrop Colgate Harper Fund in Memory of Francis P. Harper. The interest from these endowments was restricted to the purchase of Americana in five different categories and allowed the Society to buy some of the rarest and choicest pieces of early Americana. As the 1958 *Annual Report* stated, "Thus have these kind friends of the Society handsomely aided in the purchase of Americana and rare books, in perpetuity." When a rare cache of William Bradford imprints appeared in the late 1970s and early 1980s, it was to the Harper bequest that the Society turned.

Manuscripts, the primary sources of much historical research for most eras of American history (until the advent of the computerized file), continued to come into the Society. The number astounds even the most jaded collector and we can only mention a few highlights. Taking first place among manuscripts during these years was the donation of Charles II's letters patent to Governor Edmund Andros authorizing him to take New Netherlands from the Dutch in 1674. This is one of the founding documents of New York history. We mentioned above the gift of the Rufus King and family letters and library. His contemporary, Robert R. Livingston (1746–1813), was a schoolmate and law partner of John Jay, a delegate to the Continental Congress who helped draft the *Declaration of Independence*, and chancellor of New York State (1777–1801). Livingston administered the presidential oath of office to George Washington in 1789. He was Thomas Jefferson's minister to France, where he took part in the negotiations for the Louisiana Purchase. He held a number of other offices and was very active in state politics as a Republican anti-Federalist, anti-Hamiltonian. He also supported Robert Fulton's steamboat enterprise, gaining a New York monopoly for himself and Fulton. Almost all of his family papers and many of his personal effects were eventually inherited by a distant relative, Goodhue Livingston of New York City. The collection contained many important portraits, furniture (including some important Duncan Phyfe pieces), silver, and a large gathering of manuscripts.

Mr. Livingston, after negotiations with President Fenwick Beekman, decided to donate the bulk of the collection to the Society, including most of the portraits and all the manuscripts. The latter included a mouth-watering horde of excellence: important letters from Washington, Jefferson, Franklin, John Adams, Hamilton, Madison, Monroe, Baron von Steuben, Marquis de Lafayette, John Paul Jones, Thomas Paine, Philip Schuyler, James Duane, Horatio Gates, Nathanael Greene, Aaron Burr, Albert Gallatin, Rufus King,

Napoleon's Authorization for the Sale of Louisiana, April 24, 1803 Gift of Goodhue Livingston

John Jay, Gouverneur Morris, and George and DeWitt Clinton, among others. His letterbooks contain hundreds of his letters. His official correspondence relating to the Louisiana Purchase include Napoleon's authorization to sell the territory to the United States. Very few private collections of the time could equal such a gathering and today it would be difficult, and take many years and much money, to put together such a coherent and connected mass of material. As an aside, we must mention the long letter from the very mature nineteen-year-old John Jay to Livingston when they were schoolmates at Columbia University. In the letter Jay expands on proper comportment for success. This letter is in the outstanding Gilder-Lehrman Collection of Americana, now on deposit at the Society.

We mentioned the silver in the Livingston collection. We would be remiss in not reporting the long history of donations of silver and other decorative arts to the Society. Throughout the history of the institution, prominent New York families associated with the Society donated large quantities of valuable silver pieces. The de Peysters, Beekmans, Schuylers, and Verplancks, as well as the

Presentation salver by Lewis Fueter,
1772-1773
Gift of James Lawrence Aspinwall

Livingstons and others, are responsible for the Society's collection of New York silver, the finest such gathering in the country.

In our recitation of the Society's place in New York and America's cultural history, we cannot forget the Swedish operatic phenomenon Jenny Lind and "Lindomania." In the early nineteenth century many theatres still carried a less-than-respectable reputation, given that the third tier in theatres and musical halls was where prostitutes gathered. The presence of such activity kept the more respectable women out of these theatres. Along came the incomparable P.T. Barnum, who noticed that women were concerned with dramatic content as much as being seen in society. Barnum banned prostitutes from his establishments. (The Park Theatre made the third tier into the "Family Circle" in 1848 but few other theatres followed suit at the time.) In 1849 Barnum brought the Swedish singer Jenny Lind to the United States. Lind made her debut in Berlin in 1844 and became a sensation all over Europe. Barnum mortgaged all he had, paid her $150,000-plus, and brought her over for an American concert tour. Arriving in 1850 and giving her first concert at New York's Castle Garden, Lind was an immediate success. Both the "Swedish Nightingale" and Barnum reaped unprecedented earnings, and Lind became one of America's first celebrities. This goes by way of saying that Society friend Leonidas Westervelt, an avid Lind fan, gathered an unsurpassed collection of thousands of pieces of material relating to her career and donated it to the Society, making it an incomparable study center for the Lind phenomenon. With the Society's wonderful sheet music collection the West Side of Manhattan becomes the place to be for the study of music when we remember that not far away is the great Music Division of the New York Public Library at Lincoln Center, as well as the archives of the Metropolitan Opera and New York Philharmonic.

James Hazen Hyde graced the Society with his unique collection of over 800 sixteenth and seventeenth century engravings and woodcuts showing symbolic representations of the four continents. Circus buffs and popular culture researchers have long been familiar with the Society's riches concerning life under and around the big top. The collection of circus posters numbers over 1,500. Most of these posters came from James G. Strobridge of the eponymous lithographing company, who presented the Society with the nucleus of this collection in the 1950s. These colorful items, mostly from 1885 to 1930, represent all the most famous circus companies of the time, including Barnum & Bailey, Ringling Brothers, Forepaugh & Sells, and Buffalo Bill's Wild West show. Actors, magicians, motion pictures, operettas, and other acts are represented in a number of theatrical sheets. With the library's extensive holdings of circus

Barnum & Bailey Circus
Poster by Strobridge Lithographing
Co., 1897
James G. Strobridge Collection

books and ephemera, nothing remains wanting for the history of that popular institution.

The Society acquired too many prints of city views to mention during this period of abundance, but we can safely say that besides its natural focus on New York views, the entire United States is represented. We come upon lithographs of New Orleans, Cincinnati, Bangor, St. Louis, Harrisburg, Philadelphia, Jersey City, Hoboken, Charleston, Chicago, Milwaukee, Seattle, and many other locales.

Portraits of prominent Americans form another body of the Society's graphic arts collection. Businessman and discerning collector of Americana, Henry O. Havemeyer (1876–1965) was a trustee of the Society until his death. He collected and gave to the Society approximately 3,500 prints during his lifetime. Noteworthy are the many depictions of American statesmen and leaders. His collection includes 700 portraits of Washington, 250 of Lincoln, and almost 300 of Andrew Jackson, as well as vice presidents, cabinet members, Supreme Court justices, and others. Researchers have used these materials for a broad range of studies in history, biography, portraiture, iconography, and printing techniques.

We mentioned the pioneering collection of photography in an earlier chapter of this work. These years saw, however, an abundance of photograph collections coming into the Society, which documented all phases of New York life. We will only mention a few. Photographer Richard Lawrence (1858–1936) was an antiquarian collector, a member of the Grolier Club and the Society of Iconophiles, and an early member of the Society of Amateur Photographers of New York. He took a number of photographs of Lower East Side slum conditions for Jacob Riis, who published his work in his famous book *How the Other Half Lives* (1890). In fact, it has recently been shown that a number of photographs credited to Riis were actually shot by Lawrence. Lawrence also took photographs of opium smokers, prisoners at a police station, and action shots at baseball games at the Polo Grounds in 1886. In 1950 Lawrence's widow, Jessie Cort Lawrence, presented the Society with 202 copy film negatives and 186 modern reference prints of her husband's work.

What would New York be without its subways? The Society can illustrate exactly what neighborhoods looked like along many of the subway routes before the advent of underground transportation. The Board of Transportation of New York City gave the Society in 1950 approximately 50,000 photographic prints of the construction of this most necessary means of city transit. The Board of Rapid Transit, the Public Service Commission, and successor bodies systematically documented the neighborhoods before construction began, as well as the underground tunneling, subway stations, sewer reconstruction, and other subjects and locations for Manhattan, Queens, Brooklyn, and the Bronx. The photographs date mainly from the beginning of construction through 1920. Most of them are meticulously dated and identified by the subway route, providing the researcher with a systematic survey of the neighborhood buildings and everyday life along the subway lines.

Subway construction, West Fifty-ninth Street Circle
Photograph, 1900
Gift of the Board of Transportation of New York City

When the transportation went underground, many of the elevated trains became dangerous for passersby underneath. Prominent businessman and civic leader Norvin Green compiled a documentary record of 4,000 photographs of the demolition of New York's elevated railroads. Most of these lines were taken down around 1940–1941. He also had approximately 650 photographs of all the Manhattan lines and other historical photos of railroads in the early part of the century. He donated these valuable resources between 1940 and 1951.

Frederick H. Smyth was fascinated with fires and he collected about 375 photographic prints and a like number of negatives of New York City fires. Famous ones such as the 1911 Triangle Shirtwaist Company disaster are included, as well other, less notorious conflagrations. He also documented in film the development of firefighting equipment. These photographs, depicting scenes from ca. 1900 to 1920, were given by Robert E. Logan in 1958.

The last gathering of photographs we will mention here is the Doris Ulmann collection. Ulmann (1882–1934) photographed prominent people and studied with Clarence H. White early in the century—his soft pictorial style shows in her work. She photographed such notables as Calvin Coolidge, Martha Graham, and Edna St. Vincent Millay. Later she branched out and her photographs of African-Americans in Kentucky and South Carolina documented a disappearing way of life. The collection comprises the largest known body of prints made by the photographer herself, with many signed. These photographs were given by the Doris Ulmann Foundation in 1954.

We are not forgetting the large number of paintings that came the Society's way in the first sixty years of the twentieth century. The usual stream of portraits are too numerous to count. The most impressive collection that came in was the Robert L. Stuart collection of over 240 European and American paintings, and even an eighteenth century Brussels tapestry. Stuart (1806–1882) was a wealthy businessman (a candy merchant) who was the first to successfully refine sugar with steam. Later he devoted his business solely to sugar refining. In 1872 he retired and became one of New York's active philanthropists, assuming the presidency of the American Museum of Natural History and the Presbyterian Hospital, among other offices. He gave large sums of money to educational and religious

Friends
Photograph by Arnold Genthe [n.d.]
Purchased from the Genthe estate

institutions and collected a magnificent array of paintings which he gave to the Lenox Library (later the New York Public Library). We may ask why the Society took more European paintings in when the focus was, by this time, solely on Americana, but the collection also included paintings by the Americans George Bellows, Frederic Church, Thomas Cole, Asher Durand, George Inness, William Sidney Mount, and other luminaries of American art history. The one problem was that the collection was the property of the New York Public Library, which because it could not legally give it, deposited the paintings in 1944. The Society and its public still enjoy these paintings. With the Reed and Bryan collection, the Stuart paintings added to the prestige of the museum and also provided another splendid example of art collecting before the advent of professional connoisseur advisors.

It is obvious from the above narrative that the Society and its staff were great collectors of materials that would enrich the study of all facets of Americana, and we have only skimmed the surface of collecting activity during these exciting years. It is easy to criticize for acquiring too much, but simply put, collectors collect, and the great ones do so with passion and sometimes obsession. Informed collecting is what makes an institution great. The difficult part is to make accessible and care for what has been collected, and here the Society fell behind in its efforts, owing to lack of the trinity of space, staff, and funds. But it did begin to take measures to refine the collections.

The first, largest, and most obvious choices for refinement were the vast Egyptian collections and the pre-Columbian pieces. The 1805 charter and early collecting policy never said anything about ancient Egypt or the Mid-East, but the Nineveh marbles and Abbott collection did bring positive media attention to the Society and serve as its first blockbuster exhibition in the nineteenth century. They took up a large amount of space, and in the twentieth century the publicity about them was less than positive. In 1941 the indomitable and overpowering City Parks Commissioner Robert Moses criticized the Society for "mustiness," in need of revivification, and exhibit duplications with other city museums—especially the duplication of Egyptology in the Metropolitan, Brooklyn, and New-York Historical Society museums. Not many people, much less institutions, stood up to the master builder, but the Society did. The *New York Times* reported on March 4, 1941:

The New-York Historical Society registered yesterday the most vigorous protest of all the city's museums and kindred institutions criticized by Park Commissioner Moses . . . In his report to Mayor LaGuardia . . . Mr. Moses singled out the New-York Historical Society as the one institution that was "dead." In its reply to [Moses] the society disclosed a great deal more animation than some of the other institutions belabored by Mr. Moses . . .

Director Alexander Wall challenged the commissioner with his obvious lack of knowledge about the Society. Wall stated, "This society is a research institution in American history with a library of books, maps and manuscripts to which the Park Department is continually sending its research workers because its own records are insufficient to determine the facts." Wall delivered the coup de grâce to Moses's informational self-esteem when he said, "His statement that the society had Egyptian objects . . . indicates that it is a long time since Mr. Moses or anyone else representing him was here, because this collection was transferred to the Brooklyn Museum in 1937." Yes, that is correct, the sacred bulls had already moved to Brooklyn. In 1936 the Brooklyn Museum director asked that the Society deposit the Egyptian collection with his institution. Since the Society was then planning the additions to the Central Park West building and needed all the space it could get for Americana, the Society agreed on the transfer not only of the Egyptian artifacts but also the Nineveh marbles, the pre-Columbian artifacts, and the collection of weapons and materials of the Indians of the Western Plains. In 1947 the Brooklyn Museum purchased the collections. Mr. Moses eventually visited the Society and (grudgingly, perhaps) admitted the value of historical collections.

Staff at the Society was always insufficient for its needs. Alexander Wall, with the title of director since 1937, brought the institution into the twentieth century world of historical research. He also introduced and improved the Education Department, which along with scheduling lectures, worked with city schools and helped organize traveling exhibits. On April 14, 1944, Wall died in office after forty-six years of service as assistant librarian, librarian, and director. He was present during the greatest growth of the Society's collections and physical plant, and made numerous other contributions to history and bibliography.

On June 20, 1944, the Board of Trustees chose R.W.G. Vail as his successor. Vail was a prominent bibliographic scholar who worked at the American Antiquarian Society, and when chosen for the directorship was state librarian of New York. President Fenwick Beekman and R.W.G. Vail presided over the 150th anniversary of the Society in 1954. The outstanding gift of the Duke of Newcastle's copy of Robert Havell's double-elephant folio of Audubon's *Birds of America* brought rightful attention to a century and a half of collecting activities. This birthday party is well chronicled in Vail's history of the Society, *Knickerbocker Birthday*.

In 1956 James J. Heslin was appointed librarian and assistant director. In the same year the distinguished librarian of the John Carter Brown Library, Lawrence Wroth, was brought in to study the library and make suggestions for its improvement. Wroth, coming from a library with a very narrow focus (early Americana, and today still counting only 55,000 volumes), criticized the Society for its "unchecked, uncritical accumulation of materials" and especially for lacking a collection development policy. The Society took the latter point to heart, while not publicly agreeing with the former. At the end of Vail's tenure in 1959, the Society issued a collection development policy based on the Wroth report. The policy built and restricted acquisitions to the library's major strengths in Americana, with a special focus on New York State and City and their place in the American experience. Although this focus was always emphasized, the policy's tone was one of refinement and consolidation. The Society prepared to enter a new, more limited collecting era.

Chapter 4
Acquisitions, Fiscal Crisis, and Renewal
1960–2004

During the 1954 sesquicentennial celebration, President Fenwick Beekman gave a speech that summarized well the Society's past and discussed future directions for its collections. First, he mentioned the great growth of the library in the nineteenth century, whereas the museum expanded slowly due to the influx of natural history specimens and other materials eventually deemed inappropriate to the collections. He then went on to explain and justify the acceptance of the Egyptian and European holdings—the Society was the only museum in the city at the time and not saving these valuable artifacts would betray the public trust. As we have chronicled above, the Society transferred many of these collections to more appropriate museums and Beekman hinted at future disposals of out-of-scope materials. He stressed the educational mission of the Society and then discussed the future of the research library. He lamented the fact, reiterated by collectors and dealers throughout the latter half of the twentieth century, that good materials were becoming more and more difficult to acquire. Many of the valuable items were already in institutions and modern manuscripts (handwritten) were disappearing because of automation. By automation he meant the typewriter and stenographer! Today, of course, typewritten manuscripts themselves are rare and we are in an even deeper predicament with the collecting of electronic files that tend to disappear or become inaccessible because of software and hardware innovations.

Beekman was right, however, in the fact that the age of heroic collecting, the accumulation of huge collections all at once, had largely passed, except for rare exceptions. To be sure, good material still came on the market, but usually in individual pieces. The astute and informed collector could still survey collections and be ready to pounce on an item that came on the market for sale. The relationship between the dealer and collector, always of prime importance, became even more critical during these times. A good dealer will try to place the right book in the right hands, and all institutions depend on this relationship. The lifeblood of the institution still depended on donors for its support, especially in the area of highly priced manuscripts and art objects. The Society entered its 151st year confident that it could still compete among other institutions for research and museum material, and for most of the rest of the century it was successful.

James J. Heslin took over as director in 1960 and spent twenty-two years at the helm, working his first two years under Leroy Kimball, and then twenty years under Frederick B. Adams (1963–1970) and Robert G. Goelet (1971–1987). For the most part, these years were fruitful. Adams (1910–2001) was one of the most celebrated bibliophiles of the age. He became the second director of the Pierpont Morgan Library in 1948, succeeding Morgan's own librarian, Belle da Costa Greene, and remained at the Morgan until 1969. As soon as Adams took over as president he launched a capital fundraising campaign to install air-conditioning, a new ventilation system, and other measures to protect the collections. Adams was energetic and successfully raised approximately two-thirds of the money needed for the renovations, which began in 1966. The other third of the needed money came from the reserves. This outlay depleted the treasury and caused concern about future funding. The Board of Trustees adopted a "total return" policy at the same time, which allowed the Society to spend up to five percent of its endowment annually. This new policy proved to be a windfall for the Society's programs until the growth in spending outpaced incoming revenue. The economic and energy crises of the 1970s would bring the Society, and many other institutions depending on endowments, into deep deficits that would call for new strategies. For most of Heslin's directorship, however, new programs were initiated and new acquisitions burnished the Society's reputation.

With the additional monies, the Society added new public programs such as more Sunday afternoon concerts, educational programs, and larger exhibits. Attendance at the Society increased dramatically, reaching an all-time high of 109,000 in 1968. The Society also rightly broadened its acquisitions policy to include more contemporary works. Although this new approach to collecting went against the recommendations of the Wroth report, the Society felt it should move boldly through the twentieth century and acquire recent writings on New York history. Any large and valuable special research collection consists of a core of intrinsic rarities surrounded and bolstered by less rare, but still scholarly resources, and depends on subject intensive collecting. The Wroth report came from the core–intrinsic rarity school, but a large research institution such as the Society would wither under such a policy and not serve its scholarly ends and public needs.

Robert G. Goelet succeeded Adams in 1971. Goelet, descended from a Huguenot family dating back to its American arrival in 1676, was president of the Goelet Realty Company and chairman of the R.I. Corporation. We have already mentioned John Jacob Astor's avid pursuit of Manhattan real estate. While Astor was buying up land, the Goelet family was acquiring much of what Astor didn't. The great rise in the family's real estate fortune dates to Peter Goelet (1727–1811), a New York merchant. He was no upstart like Astor, however; his grandfather, Jacobus Goelet, was raised by Frederick Philipse. Philipse, as all students of early New York should know, secured an estate in the seventeenth century of all the land between Spuyten Duyvil and the Croton River; part of this land was formally erected into a manor in 1693 and Frederick then became "lord of the manor" and an influential player in early New York colonial politics. But we digress. Peter Goelet and his heirs were now the second largest real estate owning family in New York after the Astors.

Robert Goelet was an energetic collector of silver and prints, as well as one of New York's leading philanthropists. He was chairman of the American Museum of Natural History, and active in the New York Zoological Society, the National Audubon Society, and other organizations. He was the first president of the Society who gave the museum prominence (as opposed to the library) and under him the Society hired a number of skillful curators, staged exciting exhibitions, and published scholarly catalogues of the museum collections. Up to this point we have mentioned the donation of a number of art collections to illustrate the wealth and richness of the museum collection. We cannot, however, enumerate in any detail all the paintings in the collections, so we refer the reader to two definitive works that were published under Goelet's presidency: former Society museum curator Richard J. Koke's three-volume *American Landscape and Genre Paintings in the New-York Historical Society* (1982) and the *Catalogue of American Portraits in the New-York Historical Society* (1974). To emphasize the quality of the painting collections we quote from the Society's 1972 annual report:

> During the 168 years which have passed since John Pintard's Society was founded, the collection of American portraits has grown in significance and is now one of the finest in the nation. It contains likenesses of the great and near great as well as those of humble and quiet background and it represents the work of artists both famous and little recognized.

View of Hudson River, Near Sing
Sing *(New York)*
*Painting by Robert Havell, Jr.,
ca. 1850*
*Purchased from the John Jay
Watson Fund*

Let us mention just two of the many paintings acquired during this period that are indicative of the quality of the collections. William Holbrook Beard's painting, *The Bear Dance*, or *The Bears of Wall Street Celebrating a Drop in the Stock Market*, is one of the most widely produced paintings in the Society. Beard's companion study of 1879, *The Bulls and Bears in the Market*, was purchased in 1971 with money from the Bryan Fund (proceeds from the sale of out-of-scope European paintings). In the same year the Society acquired a major example of Hudson River landscape painting by Robert Havell, *View of the Hudson River, Near Sing Sing*. This painting was bought out of the Abbott-Lenox Fund (proceeds from the sale of the Egyptian and Assyrian collections) and accompanies Havell's *View of the Hudson from Tarrytown*

89

The Bulls and Bears in the Market
Painting by William Holbrook
Beard, 1879
Thomas J. Bryan Fund

Heights, donated in 1846. Havell, we must remember, engraved Audubon's *Birds of America.* In the decorative arts department the Society received in the early 1980s the wonderful Tiffany lamp collection of Dr. Egon Neustadt, as well as excellent examples of china, porcelin, silver, and other rare works.

The Society filled two very important functions during this period. The large and small exhibitions were successful in attracting media attention and in building public support for the institution, while the detailed catalogues reflected the scholarly activity that went on quietly year-by-year that made a lasting contribution to the life of the mind. Goelet's museum initiatives paid off in attendance figures as well. In 1971, 136,324 people visited the Society; in 1973, 351,727—an increase of 172 percent in two years! All the Audubon watercolors were displayed together for the first time and a new Library Gallery was unveiled to showcase specific items. The Appendix to this book contains a listing of all exhibitions from 1954 to 2004.

Growth of the works on paper continued during these years. Perhaps the largest collections acquired through purchase and gift at the time were photograph and graphic holdings, while the book acquisitions, except for a few, were not large gatherings but usually rare and often unique, and the manuscripts singular and significant.

In the photograph department, the Society followed its policy of building on strength and filling the holes in the collection by purchasing eighty photographs documenting the subway construction along Sixth Avenue. These fascinating photos accompany the large subway collection mentioned in the last chapter. And while we are on the subject of transportation, we must mention the Fifth Avenue Coach Company Photograph Collection acquired in 1981.

This company provided bus service in Manhattan from 1885 to the 1950s. Along with photographs of double-decker buses, we see public-relations photographs of employee facilities, training photographs, and the development of bus design through the years. The 920 negatives in the Billboard Photograph Collection the Society purchased in 1982 provide a fascinating view of outdoor advertising during the 1920s and 1930s. In certain cases we see monthly photographs of the same billboard that allow the historian to document changes in the neighborhood, as well as in advertising taste. Most heavily photographed locales are the Times Square area, 125th Street in Harlem, and Eighth Avenue at 110th and Third Avenue at 166th Street in the Bronx.

New York stockbroker Herman Liberman photographed almost one thousand houses of worship in New York. In four volumes he included photographs of Christian churches, Jewish synagogues, and Buddhist and Hindu temples. For seven years, from 1966 to 1973, the year of his death, he walked the span of Manhattan photographing every house of worship he found in the borough. This gift also included Liberman's photographs of the World Trade Center construction (so important for historians after the Twin Towers' destruction by terrorists on September 11, 2001) and private residences, as well as eighty prints, chiefly etchings, of buildings around Wall Street.

Another collection that documents the development of New York City is the McLaughlin Air Service Collection. In approximately 800 negatives and prints, we see New York City, primarily in 1940–1942 before postwar growth, taken at low altitudes by this air service. Such interesting urban development views as the construction of the large Parkchester Housing Project stand out.

One other photograph collection we will mention, as it complements beautifully the architectural record collection, is the Winston Weisman Collection of Architectural Photographs. Weisman, an architectural historian, documented through his photos the SoHo cast-iron architecture, Rockefeller Center, and the buildings of George Post, among other subjects. Other city buildings photographed included those in Chicago and Philadelphia. These 3,500 photographs, 3,800 negatives, and other material were taken mainly from 1950 to 1970, and donated to the Society by Weisman in 1975–1986.

The graphic art collections were enriched during this period, primarily through selective purchases and gift, but also from the donation of a few exceptional large collections. The maritime history of the United States figures prominently in a number of the print collections. A most significant gift was was the Irving S. Olds Collection of Naval Prints. Olds (1887–1963), chairman of U.S. Steel from 1940 to 1952, bequeathed to the Society a large collection of material, which included some 400 naval prints. Nearly all are in color and a large number depict engagements from the War of 1812. The Olds collection bolstered the Society's strong maritime collection, fitting for the site of such a significant world port as New York. The Naval History Society Collection, for example, contains numerous prints of ships, battles, and heroes of the United States Navy. Some significant naval prints include Joseph Frederick Wallet des Barres's *The Phoenix and the Rose*, from the *Atlantic Neptune*, which illustrates the first major naval action of the American Revolutionary War; and Edward Savage's pair of views, *Action between the Constellation and L'Insurgent* and *Constellation & L'Insurgent—The Chace* (1799).

We must mention, while on the subject of the *Atlantic Neptune*, that the British government after World War II gave to the Society the four copper plates from the *Neptune* of the scenes depicting the New York region. Additional maritime material includes posters, advertisements, and ephemera concerning the Hudson River Day Line, a shipping company that plied the waters between Albany and New York City. The Randall J. Le Boeuf collection of Robert Fulton material, donated in 1976, is replete with engravings and lithographs related to Fulton and his enterprises, including the steamboat Clermont (mistakenly named by Fulton's first biographer after Robert Livingston's estate—Fulton himself named the boat the North River Steamboat). The lithograph by F. Berthaux of *A View of West Point* reveals a rare contemporary view of Fulton's most famous

Novi Belgii Novaeque Angliae nec non Partis Virginiae Tabula . . . Multis in Locis Emendata
Map by Nicolaes Visscher, 1651–1655
Gift of Irving S. Olds

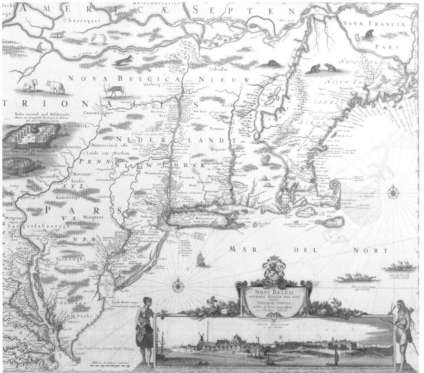

92

invention. This collection also contains 112 Fulton letters, as well as letters written by Stephen Decatur, Henry Clay, Robert Morris, Robert R. Livingston, Albert Gallatin, John Quincy Adams, and James Madison, making the Society's collection of Fulton material superior to all others.

We mentioned earlier the valuable nineteenth century California collection amassed by the father and son Society librarian team of Jacob and George Moore. This gathering, so significant in its own right, continued to grow during these years. The most outstanding addition was the very rare grouping of sixty-eight lithographs, containing over 150 illustrations of gold mines and miners, San Francisco buildings, and other scenes of California life during this rich and golden period, put together by Theodore D. Judah. Included in this collection is the very rare, unrecorded *Map of the City of San Francisco*. This acquisition is a fine example of building on strength by adding important primary research resources.

Some of the manuscript acquisitions during these years were dazzling. Perhaps automation was drying up contemporary handwritten manuscripts with original signatures in favor of the typewritten page and the autopen (first extensively used by President John F. Kennedy), but older material was still to be had. One of the most outstanding gifts of the 1960s was the Van Ness collection, donated in 1966. The year 2004 is not only the bicentennial of the Society but that of the most famous duel in history, the one between Alexander Hamilton and Aaron Burr, which took place on July 11, 1804 in Weehawken, New Jersey. Hamilton's second was Nathaniel Pendleton, and his descendants gave the Society the papers relating to the duel in 1941. In 1966 and 1967 the Society completed the documentation with the papers of Burr's second, William Van Ness. The Van Ness family gave these papers to the library and we now have

Action Between the Constellation and l'insurgent on February 9, 1799
Aquatint by E. Savage, 1799
Gift of Irving S. Olds

Letter from Aaron Burr, June 18, 1804, from the Hamilton-Burr duel correspondence
Gift of Bartow Van Ness, Jr.

a more balanced view of the tragic duel. Then in 1967 Mrs. Bartow Van Ness gave the Society an important manuscript that contained Burr's "relation of facts" of 1803 which led to the affair. The Van Ness Family papers number approximately 15,000 documents in all. The Society marked Hamilton's key role in the development of America in a comprehensive exhibit from September 10, 2004 to February 28, 2005. We need not recount one of the most famous feuds of the early Republic but will solely mention that Hamilton's (perhaps suicidal) actions ensured Burr's political demise. The Society, of course, has a large collection of Aaron Burr manuscripts, with an additional fifty-five manuscripts being added in 1974. The Burr collection is significant enough that the Burr Papers project, which resulted in a two-volume edition of his papers, was housed at the Society for a number of years. In passing, we must mention that a number of projects of scholarly editions of manuscripts have either been housed at the Society (e.g., Horatio Gates papers) or have used the collections, and that the Society has always believed that making its collections accessible in printed and other formats is an important part of its mission.

We wrote above of the diary of Philip Hone and its significance for the history of New York City. Its counterpart for a later period is that of George Templeton Strong, which covers the years 1835 to 1875. Its approximately five millions words are so rich in detail about life in the city that they equal any other diary ever written by an American. Most people know his diary through the four-volume edition by Allan Nevins and Milton Halsey Thomas published in 1952. This printed edition only skimmed the surface. Strong wrote with wit, sarcasm, and intelligence, about nearly everything in the city, and we would be remiss as historians by not mentioning that he was sometimes critical of the

Society's meetings and publications. Since he thought the proper mission of the Society was in building up its library, he would be impressed at its size and quality today, and by the fact that his manuscript takes pride of place among nineteenth century materials. He was also deeply interested in music. His editors weren't, and thus one-quarter of the diary was left unpublished until prominent musicologist Vera Brodsky Lawrence made it her job to resurrect these passages in a three-volume work, *Strong on Music*, left unfinished at her death but brought up to 1862 (this last, third volume was prepared for publication by noted scholar G. Thomas Tanselle). Lawrence, who did most of her research at the Society, put Strong's diary entries in context by researching every contemporary newspaper and other account of musical performances and controversies (newspaper music critics were especially vitriolic in those days) to produce an incomparable account of musical life in New York for the period 1835 to 1862. Her work is just one outstanding example of the important scholarship the Society's research collections make possible.

We mentioned above former Society president and stylist of the Constitution, Gouverneur Morris. In 1970 the Society purchased 134 letters to Morris from European banker Charles Jean Michel De Wolf concerning land speculation in upstate New York. It is with evidence such as this that today's historians are basing their analyses of the country's fathers' and framers' interests in land entrepreneurship and its effects on public policy. We can cite such manuscripts from a young George Washington and many others influential in affairs of state on the accumulation of land and its relation to politics in the early years of American history. Another significant manuscript acquisition at the time complements an earlier gift. This collection consists of the drafts of Morris's contemporary and New York political powerhouse Robert R. Livingston's letters to Thomas Jefferson, with one in code relating the progress of the negotiations for the Louisiana Purchase.

One of the most disturbing incidents in New York City's his-

George Templeton Strong portrait and page from Diary of George Templeton Strong, Vol. 1854–1862

Gouverneur Morris
Painting by Ezra Ames, ca. 1815
Gift of Stephen Van Rensselaer

tory came during the infamous Draft Riots in July 1863. As those informed on U.S. history know, New York rioters burned down the orphanage of the Association for the Benefit of Colored Children on July 13, 1863. In 1972 the Society received the records of this organization that span the years 1836 to 1965. The Association continued after that date as the Riverdale Children's Association. This resource is valuable for the history of African-Americans in New York, as well as that of social history and philanthropy in general. Complementing this collection was the gift in 1983 of the archives of the Leake and Watts Orphan House of Yonkers, that range from 1831 to 1949. The archive contains a large amount of material relating to that institution, as well as the Orphans Home and Asylum of the Protestant and Episcopal Church in New York, 1851–1947; the Society for the Aid of Friendless Women and Children, Brooklyn, 1869–1922; the Sevilla Home for Children, New York, 1889–1947; the Hopewell Society of Brooklyn, 1921–1947; and the Sevilla-Hopewell Society, 1947.

As we mentioned in the last chapter, New York business revolves largely around real estate, and the Society has an impressive collection of records concerning this abiding interest. In 1972 it received sixty-seven volumes of records of Trinity parish's real estate rentals between 1842 and 1902. Trinity, of course, was one of the earliest and most influential churches in New York City. Another real estate collection came from Mr. and Mrs. Charles D. Miller, who gave the Society fifty-five account books relating to the business of Frederick and William Rhinelander between 1771 and 1829. Merchants and brewers, the Rhinelanders increasingly bought up Manhattan real estate. These materials were added to Rhinelander holdings already at the Society, and another group of Rhinelander account books was given by Mrs. William Rhinelander Stewart.

To be active in any business one needs banks. Brown Brothers Harriman, founded in 1818 and the oldest private investment bank in America, gave to the Society its historical records in 1973. The collection includes over ten thousand manuscripts and 200 bound volumes on its financial matters, its early nineteenth century shipping interests, and letters concerning European ties to the Civil War, "dollar diplomacy" in Central America later on, and even material on the Truman presidency when a Brown Brothers Harriman partner was Undersecretary of State.

In 1975 the Society's Astor Family holdings were enriched by the donation of the William Waldorf Astor foundation's collection of a century's worth of records. And in 1983 Robert L. Hoguet gave a collection of letters, primarily between John Jacob Astor and Ramsey Crooks, general manager of the American Fur Company, from 1813 to 1828, concerning all facets of operations of Astor's fur busniess, the Indian trade, and other areas of Astor's affairs. Seth Low (1850–1916) was not only president of Columbia University (1890–1916) but also mayor of New York from 1901 to 1903. In 1979 the Society received the papers of the Low and related families that ranged from interests in the China trade from 1837 to 1845 to Seth Low's correspondence. The manuscripts illuminate the history of New York business, politics, and education.

To finish this short chronicle of manuscript acquisitions during these years, it is fitting and appropriate to end with the Society's founder John Pintard. In 1983 the library acquired the largest archive of Pintard material seen in fifty years. The collection contains journals, bankruptcy documents, letters, and other manuscripts relating to his imprisonment for debt. Pintard was caught up in the financial affairs of William Duer and when the latter lost his fortune through speculation, Pintard also went bankrupt because he had co-signed almost one million dollars' worth of Duer's notes. Pintard spent parts of 1797 and 1798 in jail in Newark, New Jersey. We sympathize with his plight, but we rejoice in the fact that he kept a thorough diary of his reading activities while in jail. (Duer himself spent time in debtor's prison and the Society has a broadside he published while serving his time.) Through the study of this journal we glean many insights into the reading habits of one of New York's leading citizens. We must remember that Pintard's life mirrors both New York and the Society's history during the late eighteenth and early nineteenth centuries, and these manuscripts lend support once again to this contention.

The Society has made newspaper collecting a priority since its founding and this activity continued unabated during this period. Many modern historians

Corcoran's Irish Legion, Second Regiment, Civil War recruitment poster
Published by Baker & Godwin, ca. 1862

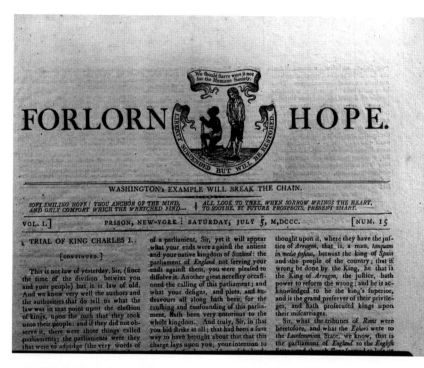

Masthead of Forlorn Hope
Newspaper, July 1800

consider newspapers second in importance only to manuscripts for their research. To mention only one example of a newspaper acquisition during these years, in 1966 the library gained an almost complete run of *The New York Clipper*, from 1866 to 1900. The *Clipper* was the oldest sporting and theatrical publication in the country.

Rare and important maps continued to come in to the collections. The seventeenth century was the golden age of Dutch cartography, and New York's Dutch origins led the Society to collect maps from this period. The library holds many, if not most, of the outstanding examples of these collaborations between cartographer, engraver, and printer, but as usual, very few collections are complete, and when an important and relevant map comes on the market, the collector is ready to stike. During these years, some gaps were filled with significant acquisitions. For instance, in 1980 the library acquired Johannes van Keulen's 1685 sea chart of New Netherland, and in 1981 the important Goos map with the first mention of the Hudson River. Also acquired was an early edition of Anthony Jacobsz's "Pascarte van Nieu Nederlandt, Virginies, Nieu Engelant an Nova Francia." Jacobsz had an important position in the group of Amsterdam publishers who specialized in maritime works. After Jacob Colomb, he was the second to publish a pilot guide with charts in the classical shape introduced by the Blaeu family. This chart is number twenty-eight from the first edition (1666) of Jacobsz's sea atlas, *Nieuw Water-Werelt*, and offers an early and curious rendition of Long Island as divided into two islands, and a larger-than-life Manhattan with the inscription, "Nieu Amsterdam ofte Manhates."

In the book department, the Adams and Goelet presidencies saw an influx of mostly individual treasures, with a few outstanding collections thrown in.

We already mentioned above the addition of a very rare octavo edition in the original paper wrappers of the Audubon birds, acquired in 1965. Audubon issued this edition in 100 installments over the four-year period, 1840–1844, and few sets remained in the original condition as most purchasers had their sets bound for ease of use and storage on bookshelves.

Thomas W. Streeter died in 1965. Streeter had served the Society for sixteen years as a trustee, treasurer, and chairman of the Finance Committee. As all those versed in collecting Americana know, Streeter was an avid, energetic, and wise collector who amassed one of the twentieth century's premier collections of Americana. Streeter had made many gifts of rare and scarce books to the library over the years. In 1966, the year after his death, seventy titles he bequeathed to the Society were transferred to the library. For the bulk of his collection, Streeter followed that other great collector of Americana, George Brinley, and sold his collection at auction while donating funds to his favorite research institutions to buy titles on the open market. The Streeter collection filled seven auction catalogues plus an index volume, with the auction running from 1967 to 1969. The catalogue itself is now a rare reference work.

The Society was able to use the Streeter money wisely, and learned much from its timidity at the earlier Brinley sale. It purchased at the sale, among other things, two William Bradford official imprints, one containing the basic account of legal procedures in New York in 1728. One other purchase was the rarest of all. We have mentioned above the Society's manuscript signed by Napoleon on April 24, 1803 authorizing the negotiations leading to the Louisiana

A South Prospect of Ye Flourishing City of New York in the Province of New York in America
Engraving by John Harris after William Burgis, 1717–1718 Issued ca. 1719–1721 Gift of Berthold Fernow

Purchase. The treaty was completed on April 30, 1803, ratified by the United States Senate on October 20, 1803, and signed by Thomas Jefferson the next day. *The Treaty and Convention . . . Relative to the Cession of Louisiana* was printed immediately in a very small edition. Only three copies were known and Mr. Streeter had one. It is this copy that the Society bought with Streeter funds, and is a lasting memorial to a great collector and friend of the Society. It is gratifying also to recount that Thomas Streeter's son Frank followed the family tradition both in his collecting acumen and in his service to the Society, serving as trustee, treasurer, and generous donor for over twenty years.

Hall Park McCullough served many years as a trustee of the Society until his death in 1966. In 1971 his children donated a magnificent selection of his library to the Society as a memorial. Having a deep admiration for Alexander Hamilton and his place in American history, Mr. McCullough gathered a splendid collection of Hamiltoniana, which came in this gift. Included was a copy of the first edition of *The Federalist*, uncut and in the original boards, a rarity indeed as most copies (including that of George Washington) were bound. Besides copies of Hamilton's famous plans and reports on public credit, we find the first edition of his first published work, albeit anonymously in 1774, *A Full Vindication of the Measures of the Congress . . . In Answer to a Letter.*

This treatise by the precocious twenty-year-old started him on his career in New York and national politics. Many other Hamilton items were included in the gift such as his unfortunate 1800 treatise, *Letter . . . concerning the Public Conduct and Character of John Adams,* which contributed to the downfall of the Federalist Party and to his tragic death in 1804. McCullough's gift also included books of Hamilton's contemporaries, as well as fine representatives of colonial Americana. The latter included a complete copy with all the maps of the five-volume set, *Purchas His Piligrimes,* published in 1625–1626. This monumental work chronicles the voyages and travels of the exploration period compiled by Samuel Purchas. Two other choice pieces of Americana in the gift are William Wood's *New England's Prospect* (1639) and John Mason's *A Brief History of the Pequot War . . . in 1637.*

In the same year as the McCullough gift, publisher Albert Boni gave over 100 imprints by and about Walt Whitman. These include the first and second issues of the first edition of *Leaves of Grass.* Mr. Boni continued his gifts throughout his life, and a later prize from him was the 1882 edition of *Leaves of Grass* printed from suppressed plates in an edition of fifty to seventy-five copies, all autographed by Whitman as gifts to his friends.

Research material comes in all formats and some of the most interesting and fascinating materials for the history of popular culture come in the form of dime novels printed on extremely fragile and cheap paper. Few great collections of this genre exist because the paper has literally disintegrated. Mr. Edward G. Levy, a discerning collector who kept his material in mint condition, gave the library approximately 1,000 dime novels which have the name *New York*, or a specific street or section of the city, in the title or subtitle.

We have mentioned many times New York's "incunabula"—issues from the press of New York's first printer, William Bradford. The Society was especially fortunate in the 1970s and early 1980s to reap a windfall of these rare editions, many of them either donated or purchased through the beneficence of the Lathrop Harper Fund. The most outstanding acquisition of all came in 1976 and is a splendid example of the symbiotic relations between dealers in rare materials and collectors. Without such a relation, great collections are seldom built. Mr. Kenneth Nebenzahl, at this time the dean of rare book and map dealers in Americana, phoned the Society informing the director of his representation of a client with eleven 1693 Bradford imprints, four of which were unknown to historians and five recorded in only one copy. Did a doubt exist in the Society's collective mind that these gems belonged in its collections? Of course not, and they were snapped up with alacrity.

The Society acquired two more Bradfords in 1980, and then in 1982 Mr. Nebenzahl again pulled a gem out of his briefcase during the reception after the annual meeting of the Bibliographical Society of America held at the Society. This was the book *New-England's Spirit of Persecution Transmitted to Pennsilvania . . .* of 1693. We must expand a bit on this title because of its significance for

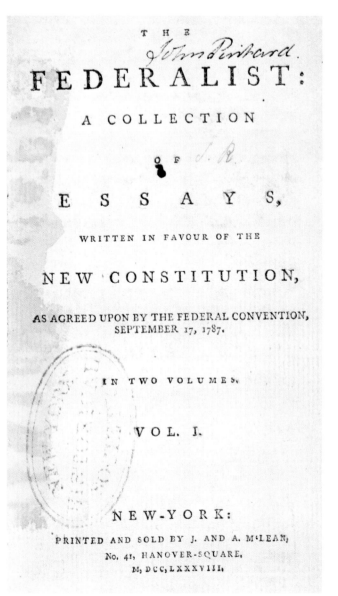

The Federalist: A Collection of Essays, Written in Favour of the New Constitution
New-York, 1787; two volumes
[Alexander Hamilton, John Jay, and James Madison]
John Pintard's copy

New York and American printing history. Before becoming New York's first printer, Bradford had been the only practitioner of his craft in Philadelphia. In 1690, however, his printing monopoly entangled him in a controversy that threatened the religious, political, and social stability of the Quaker city. The central figure was George Keith, an itinerant Quaker preacher before his immigration to New York; ever since, the controversy has borne the name the "Keithian Schism." College-educated, unlike most of his Pennsylvania co-religionists, Keith became alarmed in the late 1680s at what he considered dangerous theological imprecision among Philadelphia's less educated Quakers. To Keith's surprise, his theological criticisms quickly became a vehicle for many of the colony's craftsmen and men of lesser trades to express their opposition to the economic and political leadership of a small circle of prominent Quaker merchants. Bradford became entangled when members of each faction contracted him to print statements of their views. His involvement became personal when, to silence the opposition, the colony's authorities jailed him for four months in 1692. With the memory of his incarceration fresh in his mind, Bradford welcomed an offer from the governor and the Assembly of New York in 1693 to become "Printer to King William and Queen Mary" for the colony of New York. Safely beyond the reach of Philadelphia's authorities, Bradford published Keith's final blast without fear of retribution, probably in May, but did not print a place of publication on the treatise. All evidence, however, points to the fact that the Society purchased a copy of the first edition of the first book printed in New York, thanks once again to the Lathrop Harper Fund.

It should be obvious to the reader by now that the Society is rich in both library and museum collections. But no matter how rich the collections, if they are not accessible they are limited to a very few researchers. And up until the early 1980s, the Society was lacking in cataloguing staff, especially in the library. In 1979 the Society suffered through labor difficulties that resulted in the closing of the library. During this closing librarian James Gregory retired.

After the library reopened in 1980 the Society brought in the author of this book as its librarian. It is during these early years of the 1980s that the Society entered the computer age of bibliographic utilities and began disseminating information about the collections. We have already mentioned the library's incomparable newspaper collections—approximately 8,500 titles covering all fifty states. The National Endowment for the Humanities (NEH) began a mammoth project in the early 1980s to catalogue every newspaper ever printed in the United States. It needed a core collection of newspapers on which to base the project and thus assembled six libraries with nationwide newspaper strengths to contribute information to the database in preparation for every state to catalogue its own newspapers. The Society, along with other great institutions such as the American Antiquarian Society, received large grants to enter all their titles in this database. The Society assembled a team of four cataloguers and began work on this project in January 1983 to enter the information into the OCLC database.

In 1982 the library received another NEH grant to become a full member of the Research Libraries Group. In 1983 it began to participate in the Group's programs, particulary its computerized union catalogue, the Research Libraries Information Network. The first terminal was installed in July 1983, new cataloguers were hired, and the staff began using the system for all new and rare book acquisitions, sheet music, broadsides, and atlases. Eventually, the system would accommodate data from manuscript collections. Having access to the two major bibliographic utilities in the country, and spreading the riches electronically, brought in other funds to catalogue special collections. Andrew W. Mellon Foundation grants funded work on rare pamphlets and other collections; a U.S. Department of Education grant funded cataloguing of the Rufus King collection; the H.W. Wilson Foundation, long a supporter of the library, financed cataloguing projects on sheet music and broadsides; the Armand G. Erpf Foundation made possible the cataloguing work on the Cass Gilbert Architectural Record Foundation; and NEH has continued its funding of processing and conservation projects throughout the century. In fact, it is through cataloguing projects such as these that information about research holdings is made instantly accessible around the world, and the importance of these projects to the scholarly community is immense. In a few short years, the number of cataloguers working on the collections went from one in 1980 to over twenty in 1984. In 1980 there were 300,000 handwritten catalogue cards; by the dawn of the twenty-first century there were over 300,000 online records—a sea change in the library's accessibility. In addition, the library began digitizing its collections, completing its first project in 1999–2000. It was also in the 1980s that the

Lamp by Tiffany Studios, 1899–1920
Gift of Egon Neustadt

Society began a full-scale conservation effort for the museum collections.

In 1982 James J. Heslin retired after twenty-two years of service. The spending down of the endowment had continued during Heslin's tenure, but incoming funds didn't keep pace with expenses. Under his successor, James B. Bell (1982–1988), the Society reached the nadir of its fortunes as he accelerated the Society's fiscal decline with questionable programs and expenditures. In a sense the financial chickens came home to roost because the Society didn't raise anywhere near the necessary funds to keep it afloat. The Society's treasury was in such a financial state, especially after the stock market decline in 1987, that the endowment held a mere $7.8 million. A series of *New York Times* investigative articles in 1988 probing Bell's activities led to his resignation. By this time the Society had a new president, Albert Key (1988–1989).

Barbara Debs, a former trustee of the Society and former president of Manhattanville College, was convinced to come on board as the interim director. Debs and an advisory committee attacked the budget deficit and other problems and came up with a plan for the future, as well as a new mission statement that put a strong emphasis on education and public outreach. The trustees were pleased with her performance to the extent that Debs was appointed to the new position of president and CEO on April 12, 1989, while Norman Pearlstine, managing editor of the *Wall Street Journal*, was named chairman (the new title for the former president of the Board of Trustees). The *New York Times* reported the next day Debs's statement, "Aside from assuring financial stability and getting our collections in order, the next step is to make our collections completely available to people so that we can be an active institution in the teaching of history. We want to create more and different public programs and give the society a new look with more creative installations."

The new team had their work cut out for them. In addition to these goals, the building was badly in need of costly maintenance, requiring a heavy outlay of funds over the coming years, and the attorney general had wrapped up an investigation into the management and deaccession policies of the Society in the 1980s, an investigation that ate up funds badly needed in other areas. But the Society was attempting to get its financial house in order and it made an energetic attempt to broaden its base of support with exciting exhibitions, public lectures, and other programs. Deficits continued, however. The Board decided to look into partnerships with other institutions. In 1991 merger discussions began between the Society and the Museum of the City of New York. (Mrs. Van Rensselaer would make the proverbial turn in the grave!) The next year negotiations between the two institutions broke off. Clearly, the Society needed a plan for additional funding. On September 30, 1992, Barbara Debs stepped down as president. She accomplished much, including presiding over the raising of $20 million, reducing the deficit, and making steps toward financial soundness. She remained on the Board of Trustees.

Chairman Norman Pearlstine became acting president after Debs's departure, and investigated partnerships, first with the New York Public Library and then with Sotheby's, the auction house. The latter lent the Society $1.5 million accepting as collateral 150 museum items the staff earmarked for deaccessioning. The deal was highly controversial among the museum world when announced, but these were unusual and critical times for the Society's very existence. Even this loan was insufficient because in February 1993 the Society announced that it was trimming its staff from seventy-six to thirty-five and closing the library (the museum exhibitions had already closed down).

The main thrust of this history is on the development of the incomparable collections of the Society, and this drastic proposal was mainly aimed at saving these collections. Historians and other researchers howled when they learned of the closing of the library. But on February 19, 1993 the library closed its doors. On February 23 the city granted funds to keep the library open three days a week until April 2. An advisory committee under Wilbur Ross issued a plan to save the independence of the Society and the trustees came up with the necessary funds to keep the library open through June. But the difficulties were far from over. The Society resumed negotiations with the New York Public

Library, that if successful would move the Society's library collections to the Forty-second Street research library's facility. Before that could happen, the city and state came up with funding that would keep the Society intact and independent. With that accomplished, Norman Pearlstine resigned as acting chief executive and chairman of the Board on May 5, 1993, and Wilbur Ross and Herbert Winokur, Jr. became co-chairmen of the Society, with the latter being named acting chief executive. After fruitless negotiations with New York University to take over operations of the library with funding from the Mellon Foundation, Winokur resigned, followed by Ross in April 1994. He was succeeded by Miner H. Warner, a trustee since 1985. One of the Society's main problems during the time since Debs's departure was that it had no full-time director. This lacuna was filled on June 20, 1994 when Betsy Gotbaum, former head of the New York Police Foundation and the first female New York City Parks Commissioner, was named executive director (later president), while Warner took over as chairman of the Board.

Gotbaum reinvigorated the Society, and if not making it completely financially viable, left it with a $33 million endowment (up from $7.6 million in 1988). She knew the right people and was able to raise money and form partnerships. She had previously demonstrated her financial acumen when she ran the city parks on a reduced budget. With Chairman Warner, the Society reinvigorated the Board, reorganized the staff, and initiated a major fundraising campaign. Importantly, they retained the financial support of both the city and state. When the Society experienced its greatest financial problems in the late 1980s, the trustees stated that the Society would narrow the scope and "concentrate . . . on American history and particularly New York history." At this time many of the Society staff were put to the task of pinpointing items for deaccession. This finally came to pass in a series of auctions at Sotheby's that ran from 1995 to 1998 and saw the sale of a great many out-of-scope materials including a number of Latin American paintings, old master paintings, porcelain, excess paperweights, furniture, and other items. In the January 18, 1998 Sotheby catalogue, Gotbaum wrote a rationale for this narrowing of focus in the introduction on "reinventing the New-York Historical Society." The same year the trustees adopted a new mission statement that stated the purpose of the Society "is to collect, preserve, and interpret, for the broadest possible public, material relevant to the rich history, cultural diversity and current evolution of New York City and State and the surrounding region, as well as those collections which have important national significance." This statement narrowed even further the 1988 Board resolution and turned around 184 years of collecting policy that basically focused on New York and its larger place and impact on American history and culture. Given the nature of the library's important broad research collections (it was not for nothing that the New York Public Library desired these holdings!) and historical mission, this narrow focus would not last for very long.

One of Gotbaum's lasting legacies, however, was the creation of the Henry Luce III Center for the Study of American Culture. With a $7.5 million contribution from the Henry Luce Foundation, the Society renovated 21,000 square feet on the fourth floor of the Central Park West building to house and exhibit in a dynamic and creative way nearly 40,000 museum objects. Opening in November 2000, the Center has materials on exhibit ranging from the most valuable of paintings through dazzling silver collections, rare furniture, and Tiffany lamps, to the Rogers Groups and folk art. Study guides, labels, computerized terminals, and other educational tools give the viewer a comprehensive look at New York in all its many facets. The Luce Center's creative design allows the Society to keep on exhibit more of its rarities than ever before and is a popular educational destination for visitors to the Society.

Betsy Gotbaum's astute policies stabilized the Society and certainly brought it out of the freefall of the late 1980s and early 1990s. She began issuing published reports, beginning with 1997–1998. Much of the information contained therein recounted the partnerships with agencies and institutions she established, as well as information on grants and exhibitions. The following year, we see the reporting on collections again, the first since 1983–1984. Some exciting new collecting initiatives were reported, including the addition of the silversmith Juan Pliego (1919–2000) donation of silver. Prior to this significant addition, few pieces of twentieth century silver entered the collections. Feeling she accomplished what she set out to do, Gotbaum resigned from the Society in 2001 to run (successfully) for the position of New York City Public Advocate.

When Gotbaum resigned the Society felt the future secure enough to once again pick a scholar to run the institution. The Board's choice was Kenneth

Jackson, a prominent Columbia University historian of New York City, author of a number of scholarly works on the city, and editor of the indispensable *Encyclopedia of New York City*, a joint venture of the Society and Yale University Press, which was published in 1995. Jackson became president and CEO in May 2001 and stated that he wanted to "publicize the society's extensive research library and [suggest] novel ways to increase the institution's popularity . . ." One of Jackson's most notable achievements toward this end was his revival of the *New-York Historical Society Quarterly* under the new name *The New-York Journal of American History*. The *Quarterly*, published from 1917 until the Society's labor difficulties of 1979–1980, was the premier journal of its time devoted to New York history. The first issue of the new journal in Spring 2003 was a welcome sight and once again enriched New York's historical and scholarly landscape. Jackson's introduction to the issue reiterated the Society's historical mission to "discover, procure, and preserve whatever may relate to the history of the United States in general, and of New York City and State in particular . . ."

A good part of the initial issue of the new journal was devoted to the tragic events of September 11, 2001 when terrorists destroyed the World Trade Center and 3,000 lives, as well as crashing planes into the Pentagon and a Pennsylvania field. This defining event for twenty-first century America also led the Society to a new collecting initiative, which the first issue of the new *Journal* defined as gathering materials that

> reflect both organizational and personal response to the disaster, and include special municipal maps showing the altered downtown landscape and transit re-routings, brochures, pamphlets related to adapting to life after 9/11, signage, handwritten condolence cards and letters, photographic documentation, and World Trade Center ephemera, as well as subsequent books and publications related to the events of 9/11.

President Kenneth Jackson mobilized staff for a heroic collecting effort. The umbrella term for the Society's 9/11 program was "History Responds" and we see in the list of exhibitions in the Appendix a number of displays bearing this rubric. But "History Responds" was an all-out program that resulted in the acquisition of thousands of items ranging from oral histories, photographs, posters, and a variety of material objects relating to the disaster: steel and granite building fragments; pieces of destroyed police cars and fire vehicles; and a World Trade Center memorial of dust collected at the scene. The Society was once again taking the lead in the provision of future historical research on the city and the country.

In addition to new collecting initiatives of contemporary material to complement the other holdings, the Society scored a coup in receiving on deposit the Gilder Lehrman collection of Americana. The collection, begun a number of years ago by Richard Gilder and Lewis Lehrman, numbers over 70,000 items. Strongest in manuscripts of the American Revolution, early Federal and Jacksonian periods, and the Civil War, it contains material on all the U.S. presidents through George W. Bush. It covers such topics as exploration and expansion, slavery and abolitionism, the Constitutional Convention, the Bill of Rights, education, and many other subjects. It is not exaggerating to say that this is probably the finest private collection of Americana in the country. Gilder and Lehrman, now trustees of the Society, also fund an Institute of American History, numerous fellowships for scholars, and other activities that bring a knowledge of history closer to the public. The collection, formerly at the Pierpont Morgan Library, moved to the Society where it is housed in a specially built vault on the lower level. It is a boon to scholars having it in such proximity to the closely related vast Americana collections of the Society.

Kenneth Jackson returned to his teaching duties at Columbia University on May 31, 2003, and the next day Louise Mirrer, Executive Vice Chancellor for Academic Affairs of the City University of New York replaced him as president and CEO. Mirrer, a Stanford Ph.D. and a prominent scholar in her own right, held previous administrative leadership positions at Fordham University and the University of Minnesota. Mirrer came in with the definite goals of focusing the Society's mission on New York's place and influence on America, rather than on a more narrow local-history focus. She has high ambitions for the Society and stated that ". . . the New-York Historical Society will become known as both the preeminent institution for serious study of American history and as the locus of public engagement in, and enjoyment of learning about, the history of this country." To achieve these ends she aims to concentrate on "scholarship, with a focus on library and artistic resources; public exhibitions; and outreach to educational institutions and organizations."

World Trade Center dust
Collected from a soot-coated car
transformed into a spontaneous
memorial after it was towed from
the disaster site, September 11, 2001
Gift of Andrew Davis

The first few months of her tenure were marked by some controversy in the media, as she shifted to the broader mission of the scholarly study of American history. As mentioned numerous times above, the founders of the Society passionately embraced this broader mission, and throughout the Society's history Americana and New York's key place in the development of the country were the collecting and educational focus, and for only a few short years as a result of financial crisis did the Society ever attempt to deviate from this path. Mirrer's first great test of this broader vision was an ambitious exhibition titled "Alexander Hamilton: The Man Who Made Modern America" that opened on September 10, 2004. The largest and most expensive exhibition ever mounted by the Society, "it heralds the Historical Society's newly refashioned mission: to focus not on New York history but on national history as seen through the prism of New York," remarked the *New York Times* on September 12 . The *Times* went on to say that "if carried through as advertised, the new focus could be exactly what the city needs . . ." and quotes Louise Mirrer saying that "New York occupies a privileged place in American history, and not to have in the forefront of its consciousness that specialness would shortchange its visitors." The *Times* continued: "Lower Manhattan alone could lay claim to the title of birthplace of America. New York has never donned that mantle, but having a significant museum take on the New-York-as-America mission would be a step in that direction." Founder John Pintard would strongly agree and say, "It's about time!"

Appendix
Exhibitions
1954–2004

1954
The First Hundred Years of Columbia College
Early American Arts and Crafts
Lathrop Colgate Harper Litt. D. Spanish-AmericanWar Collection
Tom Thumb
Drawings by Baroness Hyde de Neuville
History of the New-York Historical Society
Fiftieth Anniversary of General Slocum Disaster
Watercolors of New York City Churches by Margaret Evans Price
150th Anniversary of Hamilton-Burr Duel
Treasures of the New-York Historical Society

1955
Fiftieth Anniversary of Opening of New York's Subway
Livingston Family
300th Anniversary of the Spanish and Portuguese Synagogue
American Glass
Bicentennial of Fort Ticonderoga
Colonial American Portraits and Their English Mezzotint Prototypes
The New Yorker
Arnold Schircliffe Menu Collection
Historic Bibles
Ezra Ames, Albany Artist
Christmas Story Paintings

1956
Boyd Collection of New York Etchings
The Empire State
Eat, Drink, and Be Wary
Seventh Regiment Sesquicentennial Exhibition
City Hall, New York
Presidential Campaign Cartoons
General Burgoyne
Country Houses on Manhattan Island
From Garret to Gallery
Christmas in New York

1957
Colonial and Federal Homes on Manhattan Island
French Visitors to New York, 1795–1850
River Views from the James Boyd Collection of New York Etchings
New York, City of Authors, 1760–1860
Three New York Architects, 1880–1910
George Mason and Gunston Hall
Fire Gallery
Buildings on Broadway from the James Boyd Collection of New York Etchings
Lafayette and the New-York Historical Society
Mayors of New York City, 1784–1957
Charles M. Russell: The Cowboy Artist
American Pressed Glass

1958
The Port of New York
Etchings of Buildings of Downtown New York City by James Boyd
Connecticut Valley Doorway
Nineteenth Century Carrier Addresses
DeWitt M. Lockman Memorial Exhibition
Etchings of New York City Churches by James Boyd
Portraits of the Stuyvesants

C.D. Batchelor Cartoons
Noah Webster Bicentennial Exhibition
Theodore Roosevelt Centennial Exhibition
American Daguerreotypes
America's First World's Fair
American Feminine Costumes Shown on Figurine Models
Clement Clarke Moore and "A Visit from St. Nicholas"
Miniature Models of Antique Automobiles, 1877–1914

1959
Rediscovered Painters of Upstate New York, 1700–1875
Abraham Lincoln Sesquicentennial Exhibition
The Hudson, River of History, from Lake Champlain to the Sea
Two American Naval Heroes: Oliver H. and Matthew C. Perry
American City Views by William James Bennett
Etchings by Anton Schutz

1960
Early Steamboat Advertising
Architectural Studies
The Bequest of Waldron Phoenix Belknap, Jr.
Artists' Delight and Industry's Power: Niagara Falls, 1678–1960
The Presidential Campaign of 1860: Prelude to the Civil War
Manhattan Oases: Etchings of New York City Parks and Squares
New York Theater Posters, 1870–1880

1961
It Paid to Advertise
A Nation Divided: 1861–1862
Nineteenth Century Views of New York State Communities
Civil War Military Manuals
John Hill, Master of Aquatint
American Portraits by Enit Kaufman
New York: Host to the World
Confederate School Books

1962
American Silver
The American Colonies
American Shadow Portraits
Transportation on Manhattan Island
Behind the Lines
The Second War of American Independence
The Belknap Bequest

1963
American Cities
John James Audubon and the Birds of America
Songs of the War of 1812

1964
Colorful New Yorkiana
The New York Crystal Palace, America's First World's Fair
Treasures of the New-York Historical Society, 1804–1964
The Presidential Election of 1864
New York City: Host to the World, 1679–1900

1965
Military Gallery

New York City Views: 1800–1900
The Seeds of American History: Books and Maps of Voyages and the Historic Hudson

1966
The Bequest of Waldron Phoenix Belknap, Jr.
An Exhibit of Nineteenth and Twentieth Century Glass Paperweights

1967
Maps of the Seventeenth and Eighteenth Centuries
Merchants and Planters of the Upper Hudson Valley
Theatrical Posters of Bygone Days, 1880–1920
New York in Summer
America in Allegory
Manuscript Treasures of the New-York Historical Society
Transportation in Early New York
A Visit from St. Nicholas

1968
Daguerreotypes and Their Makers: 1848–1875
Circus Posters from the Days of the Big Top
Gallery of Art
Advertising Posters from the Nineteenth Century
Central Park: Oasis in Manhattan
American Boookplates
John James Audubon: Special Expanded Exhibition

1969
Treasures of Americana
George Catlin, Artist of the American Indian
A Decade of Collecting, 1959–1969

1970
Glass Paperweights–The Collection of Mrs. F. MacDonald Sinclair
New York State and the Hudson Valley
A Visitor Looks at America
The Big Top
New York: Maritime City
Views of American Cities and Towns in the Nineteenth Century
Advertising in America
Eye on the City: The Photographer in New York, 1840–1900

1971
John Rogers's Household Gods
Audubon Gallery: John James Audubon and the Birds of America
Photographs of Nineteenth Century New York
Paint and Pattern in Rural Pennsylvania
City of Promise: Aspects of Jewish Life in New York, 1654–1970
Classics of Seventeenth Century Americana
Manuscripts from Three Centuries of American History
American Sculpture in Plaster, Wood, Metal, and Stone

1972
Two Hundred Years of Toys in America: A Guide to the Society's Collections
The American Revolution
Discovery of Independence: Maps from the Society's Collection
Road to the White House—Panorama of Presidential Campaigns
Behave Yourself: An Exhibition of Books on Etiquette and Dress from Times Past
Colonial New York
Audubon and His World

1973

Miniatures and Models
Pieter Schuyler and the Indians
Mayors of New York: 1784 to Present
New York Nostalgia
A Combined Exhibition of Colonial and Revolutionary New York
Eyewitness News of the Civil War
The Duyckincks: Merchants, Chiefs, and Painters
Gifts to the Society from Its Founder, John Pintard
New York to 1765: River, Bowery, Mill, and Beaver
New York to the Eve of Revolution
Happy Days Are Here Again

1974

Old New York in Early Photographs
Be My Valentine
Manhattan Now: Fourteen Photographers Look at the Form of the Old City
Americans in Silhouette
Verrazzano-Narrows: 1524–1974
An Exhibition of the Library's Most Cherished Treasures
New York the Empire: John Pintard and His Society
Deck the Halls

1975

Mount Pleasant–Scale Model
American Genre Painting/American Folk Art
Shaker Objects from the Collection of Edward Derning and Faith Andrews
Glass Paperweights
"Ain't I a Woman?"
"The Sword of Rebellion is Drawn": New York in the American Revolution
Joseph Raskin, Master Etcher
Jacques Reich, Master Etcher
America à la Carte: Bills of the Nineteenth and Twentieth Century
John Trumbull, Patriot Artist of the Revolution
Fordham University's John Trumbull Drawings

1976

"When in the Course of Human Events . . ."
The Declaration of Independence
History at Home: Decorative Arts of the Eighteenth and Nineteenth Centuries
The New York Cabinet Maker and His Use of Space
Words and Music: Sheet Music of Not So Long Ago
Campaigns, Conventions, and Candidates: New Yorkers and the Four-Year Itch
Op Sail: 1976
Selling New York: American Advertising from the Bella C. Landauer Collection
The Face of New York: Photographs of New York by Andreas Feininger
Two Hundred Years of American Illustration
Steamboat on the Hudson
The Dutch Republic in the Days of John Adams, 1775–1975
Moving: 300 Years of Transportation in New York

1977

The Grand Landscape: Paintings of the American Period
New York Stock Exchange: Views and Impressions
Fashions and Facades: Photographs by William Cunningham
New York Then and Now: Photographs of New York in the Past and Present
American Map Treasures, 1750–1800
Women: A Kaleidoscope from the Sophie Smith Collection

"Remember the Ladies": Women in America, 1750–1815
The Flight of the Lone Eagle
Jenny Lind and New York
The Bradford Imprints, 1693

1978
Think Small
"Give Me That Old Time Religion": Religious Ferment in Nineteenth Century New York
Street Kids
The Art of the Conservator: New Life for Old Objects
"Wish You Were Here": Nineteenth Century Resorts in New York State
The American Magazine
Over Here: World War I Posters
New York in the Forties: Photographs by Andreas Feininger

1979
The American Scene on Paper: Drawings and Watercolors from the Collection
A Child's World
Calves Heads, Eels Tartare, and Little Birds on Toast: New York Eats
The Society Collects, 1954–1979
Yesterday's View of the Future: Revisiting the World's Fair of '39
Knickerbocker Birthday: An Irreverent View of the New-York Historical Society
Artists and Architects of the New York Subway
By a Child's Hand Wrought

1980
A Panorama of Presidential Elections
55 Wall Street: A Working Landmark
Tiffany Silver
That Belmont Look
A Remnant in the Wilderness: New York Dutch Scripture Painting
The Phrenology of the Land: How to Read the Topography of New York Province and State
The Drypoints, Etchings, and Color Drypoints of Mort Imerborne
New York: Art on the Road
Small Folk: A Celebration of Childhood in America
The White Mountains: Place and Perception

1981
New York in Aerial Views
The Society of Illustrators: Twenty Years of Award Winners
Of the Land's Bounty: The Gardens, Woods, and Meadows of New York Province and State
Two Hundred Years of Freemasonry in New York
An Acre Revisited: Music from the Collection of the New-York Historical Society
The Mayor's House: Gracie Mansion and Other Dwellings
Tales of Christmas Past

1982
A Brief and True Relation: Colonial Americana from the Collections of the New-York Historical Society
George Washington in New York State: The Revolutionary War and the Presidency
MTA Photographs from the Fifth Avenue Coach Company
Sailing Ships in Dutch Prints: Four Centuries of Naval Art from the Rijks Museum
Cast with Style: Nineteenth Century Cast-Iron Stoves from the Albany Area
FDR: A Centennial Exhibition
Manhattan Observed: Fourteen Photographers Look at New York, 1972–1981
Grand Central Terminal: City within the City
The Female Touch: The Ladies' Periodicals as a Reflection of an Age
Oom Pah Pah: The Great American Band
A Collector's Sampler: Library Accessions, 1980–1982
The Birth of New York: Nieuw Amsterdam, 1624–1664

Greeting of the Year
A Sampler of American Advertising from the Bella C. Landauer Collection

1983

John Rogers's Household Gods
A Heritage to Remember: The Black Experience in New York
Aspects of American Culture
A Celebration: American Landscape Painting, Genre Art, and Drawing
The Sage of Sunnyside: A Washington Irving Bicentennial Celebration, 1783–1983
A Bridge Opens to Brooklyn
Artists' Views of Central Park: 1814–1914
A Celebration of Opera in Nineteenth Century New York: An Exhibition in Honor of the Met's 100th Birthday
Struggle for a Continent: Francis Parkman's "France and England in North America"
Firefighting on Parade
New York Themes: Paintings and Etchings by William Meyerowitz and Theresa Bernstein
The Library of John Pintard: Book Collecting in the New Republic
Lights, Camera, Action: New York's Silent Film Studios
Shanties to Skyscrapers: Robert Bracklow's Photographs of Early New York

1984

New York and the China Trade
The Sons of St. Patrick: The Irish and Irish Organizations in New York
The Adirondacks: A Wilderness Preserved
The Cultural Pleasures of Eighteenth and Nineteenth Century New York: A Centennial Tribute to the Grolier Club
The Waldron Phoenix Belknap, Jr. Collection
Five New York Families
Treasures of Manuscript Americana
Visions of Liberty
Lost in a Shuffle: Playing Cards and Board Games from Bygone Days
Ardent Spirits and Demon Rum: Temperance Movements in America
The City Comes of Age: The Society Reminisces on Its 180th Birthday
Her Voice Was Heard: Women and Politics in America
A Pageant of Heraldry in Britain and America
The Baroness Hyde de Neuville: Sketches of America, 1807–1822
Lurid Literature: Popular Reading of the Nineteenth Century

1985

American Toy Books: Juvenile Ephemera
Centuries of Childhood in New York: A Celebration of the 275th Anniversary of Trinity School
Karol Kowalski: 1885–1969
John James Audubon's Birds of North America: The Original Watercolors
The Statue of Liberty: America's Symbol of Freedom in Souvenirs and Ephemera
Chicago and New York: More Than a Century of Architectural Interaction
Metropolis in Mourning: Ulysses S. Grant, 1822–1855
To the Public: New York in Broadside
Artist in Residence: The North Country Art of Frederic Remington
The Great Fire of 1835: Sesquicentennial Anniversary

1986

Niagara: Two Centuries of Changing Attitude, 1697–1901
Prized Prints
P.T. Barnum: Prince of Humbug, Merchant of Delight
Liberty's Legacy: Photographs of New York's Ethnic Festivals
James Henry Cafferty: 1819–1869
Treasures of Botanical Illustrations
Storied Shores: Lake George in Legend and History
Portraits of Power: Paintings from the Collection of the New York Chamber of Commerce and Industry
Made for New York: Antique Toys from the Lawrence Scripps Wilkinson Collection
A Portrait of Livingston Manor, 1686–1850
The Pleasure of Your Company: Parties and Balls in New York City

1987

New York Bestiary: Pets and Pests of Metropolis
The Wagstaff Collection of American Silver
Hudson River and the Highlands: Photos by Robert Glenn
Are We to Be a Nation? The Making of the Federal Constitution
Jackie Robinson: An American Journey
Strong on Music: The New York Music Scene, 1836–1850
Ex Libris Rufus King
Government by Choice: Inventing the United States Constitution
Jasper Cropsey: Artist and Architect

1988

The Blizzard of '88
Bellows, Bobbins, and Butter Churns: Keeping House in Nineteenth Century America
Francis W. Edmonds: American Master in the Dutch Tradition
Artistic Houses: Lavish Interiors of Nineteenth Century New York
The Rise and Fall of New York: Building and Unbuilding Manhattan
The Invisible Surface: Paper and the Printing Arts in Early America
Arnold Newman: Five Decades
Hard Cider and Hot Air
Celebrating the Holidays in New York
The Belknap Collection of Silver Portraits

1989

Burr McIntosh: Polite Society, 1900–1920
Hurray for Old Glory! Flag Paintings by Chil de Hassam
George Washington in New York
Irving Browning City of Contrasts
Posters by Edward Penfield
Cased Images: The 150th Anniversary, of Photography
An American Sampler: Folk Art from the Shelburne Museum
Beth Israel Hospital Centennial

1990

Calyo
Below the Line: Living Poor in America
Manhattan Contrasts: Twentieth Century Paintings of New York from the Permanent Collection
Thomas Jefferson Bryan Collection: Changing Attributions
World War II Posters
Paris 1889: American Art Expo
Charles Gilbert Hine: Impressions of a City
The Legacy of Luman Reed
Art What Thou Eat

1991

Markers of Change: Documents of American History
The Taste of Andrew Carnegie
Justice Rendered: The Courts of New York Colony and State, 1691–1991
Culinary Collection
Jewish Artists in New York
New York Architecture: NYC/ALA 1991 Design Awards
McKim, Mead, and White's New York
From New York Bay to the Erie Canal: The Watercolors of William Rickarby Miller
Landscapes of W.R. Miller
On with the Show! Circus and Theater Posters from the Collections at the New-York Historical Society
Imagining the New World:Columbian Iconography
Brooklyn Navy Yard Photographs
The Home Front in New York City

1992

The Native Americans
Dreams and Shadows: Thomas H. Hotchkiss in Nineteenth Century Italy
A Forest Forever: Art and the Adirondacks
Patronage and Collecting
Building City Hall Competition, Construction, and Context
Party Time: Presidential Campaigns Since 1832
Louis XVI Chair/Textiles
500 Years of American Clothing
Library Treasures
Hyde Collection
Stonewall Conference
William Stanley Haseltine
The Names Project AIDS Memorial Quilt: An International AIDS Memorial

1993

Victorian Pleasures
The American Discovery of Italy, 1760–1920
Sony Exhibition
Pursuit of Fame
Children's Books/Woodblocks
Architectural Drawings
Miniatures

1994

Nineteenth-Century American Masterworks from the Collections of the New-York Historical Society
Louis Comfort Tiffany Glass
Luman Reed Gallery
Reinstallation of the Permanent Collection

1995

The Grand American Avenue, 1850–1920
Thomas Cole: Landscape into History
Treasury of the Past/Treasures of the New-York Historical Society
Inventory: Christian Boltanski
Who Was Pocahontas?
Perspectives on New York: Selections from the Historical Society Map Survey
World War II Posters and Photographs
Clement Clark Moore and "A Visit from St. Nicholas"

1996

Wrought in Common Clay: A Century of New York Stoneware
New York Then and Now: The Upper West Side
In Cold Blood: Murders That Shocked New York
Cass Gilbert: Designing the American Monument
Becoming Eleanor Roosevelt: The Early New York Years, 1884–1933
Metropolitan Lives: The Ashcan Artists and Their New York, 1897–1917
SCAASI: The Joy of Dressing Up–A Retrospective
Victoria Woodhull

1997

In Search of Light: Tiffany at the Historical Society
Before Central Park: The Life and Death of Seneca Village
An Unquenchable Thirst: Springs and Wells of New York City
Feathers!
Taking Flight: John James Audubon and the Watercolors for the Birds of America
From New York to Salt Lake: The Church of Jesus Christ of Latter Day Saints
To Hell with Reform: The Race to Become Mayor of Greater New York
Photographs of John James Albok

On the Nose: Spectacles and Other Optical Fashions
Yours, Henry James
Signs and Wonders: The Spectacular Lights of Times Square
Times Square: Then and Now
"'Twas the Night Before Christmas"

1998

Designing Women: American Art Posters from the Collection
The Deuce
Militant Metropolis: New York City and the Spanish-American War, 1898
The Landmarks of New York (New York City Landmarks: Photographs)
Paul Robeson: Bearer of Culture
Unconventional Currier and Ives
Uniting Neighbors
Kid City
Fading Ad Campaign: Vintage Painted Advertisements
William Sidney Mount: Painter of American Life
George B. Post: Great American Architect
New York's Finest: A History of the New York Police Department
From Push Carts to Restaurant Deluxe: Dining in New York at the Turn of the Century
Treasures from Mt. Vernon: George Washington Revealed
Over the Door: The Ornamental Stonework of New York

1999

Eyeing the World Around Us (Photos of Students from St. Jean Baptiste High School)
Views of a Modern City: New York, 1900–1950
Secrets of a Beautiful Face: Beauty Product Advertisements from the Collection
John N. Genin: The Celebrated Hatter
Refuge: The Newest New Yorkers
Dance for a City: Fifty Years of the New York City Ballet
Yadda, Yadda, Yadda: Quotes about New York
Uncle Sam: The Image of a Nation
Building History: History Building
Presenting the Past: Glimmers of New York Silver from the Society's Collection
Putting It on Paper: 200 Years of American Drawings and Watercolors
Privy to History
$24: The Legendary Deal for Manhattan
Masterworks of Nineteenth Century American Paintings
Italians in New York: Five Centuries of Struggle and Achievement
Winter in New York: Paintings from the Permanent Collection
Bird's Eye Views of New York
Times Square in Pictures: A Century of Images

2000

Bruce Davidson: East 100th Street
John James Audubon: The Birds of Winter
New York on the Brink: The City's Fiscal Crisis of 1975
Hair!
A Quiet New York Life: Photographs from the Daniel Coleman Collection
Without Sanctuary: Lynching Photography in America
Jesse Tarbox Beals: On Assignment
Irwin Silver: Photographs
Magnum Our Touring World: Photographs, 1989–1999
The Stork Club
New York Inside Out
The Changing Face of Liberty: Female Allegories of America
Manhattan Contrasts: Twentieth Century Paintings of New York from the Permanent Collection
Gignoux Paintings Rediscovered, Conserved, and Exhibited
Fit for a King (Gouverneur Morris: Statesman and Connoisseur)

Jenny Lind: The Swedish Nightingale in America
Inventing the Skyline: The Architecture of Cass Gilbert
Strobridge Posters from the Collection of the Historical Society
Looking at History: New York After-School Spring Exhibit
Intimate Friends: Thomas Cole, Asher B. Durand, and William Cullen Bryant
Pray for Me: American Wartime Messages, 1759–1968 (The Civil War Project)
Eye of the Storm: The Civil War Drawings of Robert Knox Sneden (The Civil War Project)
Remedies for Old Age and What Else Ails You: Trade Cards from the Bella C. Landauer Collection
Elder Grace: The Nobility of Aging
The Henry Luce Center III Center for the Study of American Culture

2001
The Course of Empire
Advertising Drama: The Theater in Manhattan and the Hinterland
The Sight of Music: Prints from the Collection of Reba and Dave Williams
Night Walks: Photographs by Irwin Silver
Choosing to Participate: Facing History and Ourselves
Walkabout: Past and Present Views of New York
Out of Time: Design for the Twentieth Century Future
Lighthouses
Independence and Its Enemies in New York
Up on a Roof: The Culture of New York City Rooftops
Flophouse: Life on the Bowery
The Rosenbergs Reconsidered: The Death Penalty in the Cold War Era
Manhattan Unfurled
The British in New York
Seventy-five Years of Holiday Magic: Macy's Thanksgiving Parade
John Koch: Painting a New York Life
New York September 11th by Magnum Photographers (History Responds)

2002
In Memoriam: Chief William Feehan (History Responds)
Nadelman's Four Seasons
Family Matters: A Century of Family Business in New York
World Trade Center: Monument (History Responds)
Presidential Manuscripts at the New-York Historical Society (Presidential Treasures)
Ralph Fasanella's America
Missing: Streetscape of a City in Mourning (History Responds)
9/11 through a Child's Eye (History Responds)
In Focus: Selections from the Painting Collection
The Games We Played: Victorian Games from the Liman Collection
Building on the Flatiron: The Centenary of a New York Icon
The Tumultuous Fifties: A View from the *New York Times* Photo Archives
Me, Myself, and Infastructure
The Angry Dove: The 200th Anniversary of the June 12, 1982 Nuclear Disarmament Demonstration
9/11 by Four-Four Exhibits Below (History Responds)
The Twin Towers Remembered: The Photography of Camilo Jose Vergara (History Responds)
Pilgrimage: Looking at Ground Zero, Photographs by Kevin Bubriski (History Responds)
In the Light of Memory: A Spherical Panorama from the South Tower of the World Trade Center (History Responds)
Beyond Ground Zero: The Forensic Science of Disaster Recovery (History Responds)
Photographs of David Margules (History Responds)
9/11: One Year Later (History Responds)
Life on the Lapel: An Exhibition of Buttons, Badges, Metals, and Decoration from the Collection
Portrait of the Art World: A Century of Art News Photographs
Reading Uncle Tom's Image: A Reconsideration of Harriet Beecher Stowe's 150-Year-Old Character
Degrees of Latitude: Mapping Colonial America
Seat of Empire: Napoleon's Armchair from Malmaison to Manhattan
Home of the Free: A Student Photojournalism Project
Gouverneur Morris Treasures

Freedom: A History of Us
New York Diary: The Collages of John Evans

2003

Feiffer's Family Tree
Julz Rules: Inside the Mind of Jules Feiffer
Beals, Harvey, and Hewitt: Women Pioneers of Architecture and Design Photography
Bella C. Landauer: Collector of Enterprise
Enterprising Women: 250 Years of American Business
Celebrating a Life in Design: The Recent Gifts of Eva Zeisel
African-American Masters: Highlights from the Smithsonian American Art Museum
The Ladies Christian Union: Mrs. Marshall O. Roberts
Telling Lives
Remembering the Forgotten Ones: The Photographs of Milton Rogovin
Fathers and Children: Loss and Remembrance, September 11 (History Responds)
Petropolis: A Social History of Urban Animal Companions
Urban Oasis: The Greening of Early New York
New York: In the Light of Memory (History Responds)
Ann Zane Shanks: Behind the Lens
The Manhattan Graphics Center: 9/11 Portfolio Project (History Responds)
Children at Risk: Protecting New York City's Youth, 1653–2003
The Birds of Central Park: Audubon's Watercolors
Home Sewn: Three Centuries of Stitching History
Recovery: The World Trade Center Recovery Operations at Fresh Kills (History Responds)
Home of the Free: A Student Photojournalism Project Part 2

2004

Radical Hospitality (History Responds)
The Luman Reed Gallery: A History of Art Collecting in Nineteenth Century New York
From the Classroom to the World–Hine, Ulmann, Strand, Arbus, and the Ethical Culture Fieldston School
New Views of New York: Recent Aquisitions of New York Cityscapes
À la Carte: A Sampling of Menus from the New-York Historical Society Library Collection
The General Slocum and Little Germany
From Abyssinian to Zion: Photographs of Manhattan's Houses of Worship by David Dunlap
If Elected: Campaigning for the Presidency
Campaigns on Cotton
Around Town Underground: Prints from the Collection of Dave and Reba Williams
The Rescue (History Responds)
Hamilton: The Man Who Made Modern America

Bibliographic Note

Any great research institution and museum with a 200-year history will have a myriad of books and articles relating to its history and collections. The following references just touch the surface of the story of the New-York Historical Society. My debt to the Annual Reports of the Society for the years 1931–1984 are obvious. Anyone who wants to chronicle the annual acquisitions has to start with these indispensable sources. *The New-York Historical Society Quarterly*, from 1917–1980, is also replete with collections-based articles. For the earlier period, former director R.W.G. Vail's *Knickerbocker Birthday: A Sequi-Centennial History of the New-York Historical Society* (New York: The New-York Historical Society, 1954) is essential. The development of the library from its beginnings to the early period of this author's tenure receives sound historical treatment in Pamela Spence Richards's *Scholars and Gentlemen: The Library of The New-York Historical Society: 1804–1982* (Hamden: Archon, 1984). For the graphic art or works on paper collections, Helena Zinkham's book is comprehensive and indispensable: *A Guide to Print, Photograph, Architecture & Ephemera Collections* (New York: The New-York Historical Society, 1998). Also see Wendy Shadwell, "Prized Prints: Rare American Prints Before 1860 in the Collection of the New-York Historical Society," in *Imprint* (1986). For the Landauer Collection, see Bella C. Landauer, "Collecting and Recollecting," in the *New-York Historical Society Quarterly* (1959); and Mary Black, *American Advertising Posters of the Nineteenth Century: From the Bella C. Landauer Collection of The New-York Historical Society* (New York: Dover Publications, 1976). For paintings, the most recent and valuable books are *Catalogue of American Portraits in the New-York Historical Society* (two volumes; New Haven: Yale University Press, 1974); Richard J. Koke's *American Landscape and Genre Paintings in the New-York Historical Society* (three volumes; New York: The New-York Historical Society, 1982); and Ella M. Foshay's *Mr. Luman Reed's Picture Gallery; A Pioneer Collection of American Art* (New York: Harry N. Abrams in Association with the New-York Historical Society, 1990). For a general overview of the collections and the Henry Luce III Center, see *Perspectives on the Collections of The New-York Historical Society* (New York: The New-York Historical Society, 2000). I have also drawn on my own articles: "The Cartographic Treasures of The New-York Historical Society," in *The Map Collector* (March 1986); "The Print Collections of The New-York Historical Society," in *The Print Collector* (Autumn 1981); "Books, Power, and the Development of Libraries in the New Republic: The Prison and Other Journals of John Pintard of New York," in *Journal of Library History* (Spring 1986); and "Another Clue to Thomas Cole" (with Mary Alice Mackay), in *Arts Magazine* (January 1986). The rich manuscript collections are detailed in Arthur Breton, *A Guide to the Manuscript Collections of the New-York Historical Society* (two volumes; Westport: Greenwood Press, 1972). For an examination of the financial and other problems of the Society in the second half of the twentieth century, see Kevin M. Guthrie, *The New-York Historical Society: Lessons from One Nonprofit's Long Struggle for Survival* (San Francisco: Jossey-Bass Publishers, 1996). For the "History Responds" collecting initiative of material related to September 11, see Jan Seidler Ramirez, "Present Imperfect: The New-York Historical Society's Collecting Odyssey of 9/11/01," in *The New-York Journal of American History* (Spring 2003). So many histories of New York City exist that we cannot mention them all, but two essential sources are Edwin G. Burrows and Mike Wallace, *Gotham: A History of New York City to 1898* (New York: Oxford University Press, 1999); and Kenneth T. Jackson, editor, *Encyclopedia of New York City* (New Haven: Yale University Press, and New York: The New-York Historical Society, 1995).